ASPEN PUBLISHERS

D0817904

Casenote™ Legal Briefs

CORPORATE TAXATION

Keyed to Courses Using

Lind, Schwarz, Lathrope, and Rosenberg's
Fundamentals of Corporate Taxation

Seventh Edition

Wolters Kluwer
Law & Business

AUSTIN   BOSTON   CHICAGO   NEW YORK   THE NETHERLANDS

This publication is designed to provide accurate and authoritative information in regard to the subject matter covered. It is sold with the understanding that the publisher is not engaged in rendering legal, accounting, or other professional services. If legal advice or other expert assistance is required, the services of a competent professional person should be sought.

— From a Declaration of Principles adopted jointly by a Committee of the American Bar Association and a Committee of Publishers and Associates

Aspen Publishers
Attn: Permissions Dept.
76 Ninth Avenue, 7th Floor
New York, NY 10011-5201

To contact Customer Care, e-mail customer.care@aspenpublishers.com, call 1-800-234-1660, fax 1-800-901-9075, or mail correspondence to:

Aspen Publishers
Attn: Order Department
P.O. Box 990
Frederick, MD 21705

Printed in the United States of America.

1 2 3 4 5 6 7 8 9 0

ISBN 978-0-7355-8265-1

About Wolters Kluwer Law & Business

Wolters Kluwer Law & Business is a leading provider of research information and workflow solutions in key specialty areas. The strengths of the individual brands of Aspen Publishers, CCH, Kluwer Law International and Loislaw are aligned within Wolters Kluwer Law & Business to provide comprehensive, in-depth solutions and expert-authored content for the legal, professional and education markets.

CCH was founded in 1913 and has served more than four generations of business professionals and their clients. The CCH products in the Wolters Kluwer Law & Business group are highly regarded electronic and print resources for legal, securities, antitrust and trade regulation, government contracting, banking, pension, payroll, employment and labor, and health-care reimbursement and compliance professionals.

Aspen Publishers is a leading information provider for attorneys, business professionals and law students. Written by preeminent authorities, Aspen products offer analytical and practical information in a range of specialty practice areas from securities law and intellectual property to mergers and acquisitions and pension/benefits. Aspen's trusted legal education resources provide professors and students with high-quality, up-to-date and effective resources for successful instruction and study in all areas of the law.

Kluwer Law International supplies the global business community with comprehensive English-language international legal information. Legal practitioners, corporate counsel and business executives around the world rely on the Kluwer Law International journals, loose-leafs, books and electronic products for authoritative information in many areas of international legal practice.

Loislaw is a premier provider of digitized legal content to small law firm practitioners of various specializations. Loislaw provides attorneys with the ability to quickly and efficiently find the necessary legal information they need, when and where they need it, by facilitating access to primary law as well as state-specific law, records, forms and treatises.

Wolters Kluwer Law & Business, a unit of Wolters Kluwer, is headquartered in New York and Riverwoods, Illinois. Wolters Kluwer is a leading multinational publisher and information services company.

Format for the Casenote Legal Brief

Nature of Case: This section identifies the form of action (e.g., breach of contract, negligence, battery), the type of proceeding (e.g., demurrer, appeal from trial court's jury instructions) or the relief sought (e.g., damages, injunction, criminal sanctions).

Fact Summary: This is included to refresh your memory and can be used as a quick reminder of the facts.

Rule of Law: Summarizes the general principle of law that the case illustrates. It may be used for instant recall of the court's holding and for classroom discussion or home review.

Facts: This section contains all relevant facts of the case, including the contentions of the parties and the lower court holdings. It is written in a logical order to give the student a clear understanding of the case. The plaintiff and defendant are identified by their proper names throughout and are always labeled with a (P) or (D).

Palsgraf v. Long Island R.R. Co.

Injured bystander (P) v. Railroad company (D)

N.Y. Ct. App., 248 N.Y. 339, 162 N.E. 99 (1928).

NATURE OF CASE: Appeal from judgment affirming verdict for plaintiff seeking damages for personal injury.

FACT SUMMARY: Helen Palsgraf (P) was injured on R.R.'s (D) train platform when R.R.'s (D) guard helped a passenger aboard a moving train, causing his package to fall on the tracks. The package contained fireworks which exploded, creating a shock that tipped a scale onto Palsgraf (P).

🏛 RULE OF LAW
The risk reasonably to be perceived defines the duty to be obeyed.

FACTS: Helen Palsgraf (P) purchased a ticket to Rockaway Beach from R.R. (D) and was waiting on the train platform. As she waited, two men ran to catch a train that was pulling out from the platform. The first man jumped aboard, but the second man, who appeared as if he might fall, was helped aboard by the guard on the train who had kept the door open so they could jump aboard. A guard on the platform also helped by pushing him onto the train. The man was carrying a package wrapped in newspaper. In the process, the man dropped his package, which fell on the tracks. The package contained fireworks and exploded. The shock of the explosion was apparently of great enough strength to tip over some scales at the other end of the platform, which fell on Palsgraf (P) and injured her. A jury awarded her damages, and R.R. (D) appealed.

ISSUE: Does the risk reasonably to be perceived define the duty to be obeyed?

HOLDING AND DECISION: (Cardozo, C.J.) Yes. The risk reasonably to be perceived defines the duty to be obeyed. If there is no foreseeable hazard to the injured party as the result of a seemingly innocent act, the act does not become a tort because it happened to be a wrong as to and her. If the wrong was not willful, the plaintiff must show that the act as to her had such great and apparent possibilities of danger as to entitle her to protection. Negligence in the abstract is not enough upon which to base liability. Negligence is a relative concept, evolving out of the common law doctrine of trespass on the case. To establish liability, the defendant must owe a legal duty of reasonable care to the injured party. A cause of action in tort will be where harm,

though unintended, could have been averted or avoided by observance of such a duty. The scope of the duty is limited by the range of danger that a reasonable person could foresee. In this case, there was nothing to suggest from the appearance of the parcel or otherwise that the parcel contained fireworks. The guard could not reasonably have had any warning of a threat to Palsgraf (P), and R.R. (D) therefore cannot be held liable. Judgment is reversed in favor of R.R. (D).

DISSENT: (Andrews, J.) The concept that there is no negligence unless R.R. (D) owes a legal duty to take care as to Palsgraf (P) herself is too narrow. Everyone owes to the world at large the duty of refraining from those acts that may unreasonably threaten the safety of others. If the guard's action was negligent as to those nearby, it was also negligent as to those outside what might be termed the "danger zone." For Palsgraf (P) to recover, R.R.'s (D) negligence must have been the proximate cause of her injury, a question of fact for the jury.

▶ ANALYSIS
The majority defined the limit of the defendant's liability in terms of the danger that a reasonable person in defendant's situation would have perceived. The dissent argued that the limitation should not be placed on liability, but rather on damages. Judge Andrews suggested that only injuries that would not have happened but for R.R.'s (D) negligence should be compensable. Both the majority and dissent recognized the policy-driven need to limit liability for negligent acts, seeking, in the words of Judge Andrews, to define a framework "that will be practical and in keeping with the general understanding of mankind." The Restatement (Second) of Torts has accepted Judge Cardozo's view.

Quicknotes

FORESEEABILITY A reasonable expectation that change is the probable result of certain acts or omissions.

NEGLIGENCE Conduct falling below the standard of care that a reasonable person would demonstrate under similar conditions.

PROXIMATE CAUSE The natural sequence of events without which an injury would not have been sustained.

Party ID: Quick identification of the relationship between the parties.

Concurrence/Dissent: All concurrences and dissents are briefed whenever they are included by the casebook editor.

Analysis: This last paragraph gives you a broad understanding of where the case "fits in" with other cases in the section of the book and with the entire course. It is a hornbook-style discussion indicating whether the case is a majority or minority opinion and comparing the principal case with other cases in the casebook. It may also provide analysis from restatements, uniform codes, and law review articles. The analysis will prove to be invaluable to classroom discussion.

Issue: The issue is a concise question that brings out the essence of the opinion as it relates to the section of the casebook in which the case appears. Both substantive and procedural issues are included if relevant to the decision.

Holding and Decision: This section offers a clear and in-depth discussion of the rule of the case and the court's rationale. It is written in easy-to-understand language and answers the issue presented by applying the law to the facts of the case. When relevant, it includes a thorough discussion of the exceptions to the case as listed by the court, any major cites to the other cases on point, and the names of the judges who wrote the decisions.

Quicknotes: Conveniently defines legal terms found in the case and summarizes the nature of any statutes, codes, or rules referred to in the text.

Note to Students

Aspen Publishers is proud to offer *Casenote Legal Briefs*—continuing thirty years of publishing America's best-selling legal briefs.

Casenote Legal Briefs are designed to help you save time when briefing assigned cases. Organized under convenient headings, they show you how to abstract the basic facts and holdings from the text of the actual opinions handed down by the courts. Used as part of a rigorous study regimen, they can help you spend more time analyzing and critiquing points of law than on copying bits and pieces of judicial opinions into your notebook or outline.

Casenote Legal Briefs should never be used as a substitute for assigned casebook readings. They work best when read as a follow-up to reviewing the underlying opinions themselves. Students who try to avoid reading and digesting the judicial opinions in their casebooks or online sources will end up shortchanging themselves in the long run. The ability to absorb, critique, and restate the dynamic and complex elements of case law decisions is crucial to your success in law school and beyond. It cannot be developed vicariously.

Casenote Legal Briefs represents but one of the many offerings in Aspen's Study Aid Timeline, which includes:

- *Casenote Legal Briefs*
- *Emanuel Law Outlines*
- *Examples & Explanations* Series
- *Introduction to Law* Series
- Emanuel *Law in a Flash* Flashcards
- Emanuel *CrunchTime* Series

Each of these series is designed to provide you with easy-to-understand explanations of complex points of law. Each volume offers guidance on the principles of legal analysis and, consulted regularly, will hone your ability to spot relevant issues. We have titles that will help you prepare for class, prepare for your exams, and enhance your general comprehension of the law along the way.

To find out more about Aspen Study Aid publications, visit us online at *http://lawschool.aspenpublishers.com* or email us at *legaledu@wolterskluwer.com*. We'll be happy to assist you.

Free access to Briefs online!

Download cases from this Casenote Legal Brief. Simply fill out this form for full access to this useful feature provided by Loislaw. Learn more about Loislaw services on the inside front cover of this book or visit *www.loislawschool.com*.

Name	Phone ( )
Address	**Apt. No.**
City	**State** **ZIP Code**
Law School	**Year** (check one) ☐ 1st ☐ 2nd ☐ 3rd

Cut out the UPC found on the lower left-hand corner of the back cover of this book. Staple the UPC inside this box. Only the original UPC from the book cover will be accepted. No photocopies or store stickers are allowed.

Attach UPC
inside this box.

Email (Print legibly or you may not get access!)
Title of this book (course subject)
Used with which casebook (provide author's name)

Mail the completed form to: Aspen Publishers, Inc.
Legal Education Division
Casenote Online Access
130 Turner Street, Building 3, 4th Floor
Waltham, MA 02453-8901

I understand that online access is granted solely to the purchaser of this book for the academic year in which it was purchased. Any other usage is not authorized and will result in immediate termination of access. Sharing of codes is strictly prohibited.

Signature _____

Upon receipt of this completed form, you will be emailed codes with which to access the briefs for this Casenote Legal Brief. Online briefs are not available for all titles. For a full list of Casenote Legal Brief titles, please visit *http://lawschool.aspenpublishers.com*.

Make a photocopy of this form and your UPC for your records.

For detailed information on the use of the information you provide on this form, please see the PRIVACY POLICY at www.aspenpublishers.com.

A. Decide on a Format and Stick to It

Structure is essential to a good brief. It enables you to arrange systematically the related parts that are scattered throughout most cases, thus making manageable and understandable what might otherwise seem to be an endless and unfathomable sea of information. There are, of course, an unlimited number of formats that can be utilized. However, it is best to find one that suits your needs and stick to it. Consistency breeds both efficiency and the security that when called upon you will know where to look in your brief for the information you are asked to give.

Any format, as long as it presents the essential elements of a case in an organized fashion, can be used. Experience, however, has led *Casenotes* to develop and utilize the following format because of its logical flow and universal applicability.

NATURE OF CASE: This is a brief statement of the legal character and procedural status of the case (e.g., "Appeal of a burglary conviction").

There are many different alternatives open to a litigant dissatisfied with a court ruling. The key to determining which one has been used is to discover *who is asking this court for what.*

This first entry in the brief should be kept as *short as possible.* Use the court's terminology if you understand it. But since jurisdictions vary as to the titles of pleadings, the best entry is the one that addresses who wants what in this proceeding, not the one that sounds most like the court's language.

RULE OF LAW: A statement of the general principle of law that the case illustrates (e.g., "An acceptance that varies any term of the offer is considered a rejection and counteroffer").

Determining the rule of law of a case is a procedure similar to determining the issue of the case. Avoid being fooled by red herrings; there may be a few rules of law mentioned in the case excerpt, but usually only one is *the* rule with which the casebook editor is concerned. The techniques used to locate the issue, described below, may also be utilized to find the rule of law. Generally, your best guide is simply the chapter heading. It is a clue to the point the casebook editor seeks to make and should be kept in mind when reading every case in the respective section.

FACTS: A synopsis of only the essential facts of the case, i.e., those bearing upon or leading up to the issue.

The facts entry should be a short statement of the events and transactions that led one party to initiate legal proceedings against another in the first place. While some cases conveniently state the salient facts at the beginning of the decision, in other instances they will have to be culled from hiding places throughout the text, even from concurring and dissenting opinions. Some of the "facts" will often be in dispute and should be so noted. Conflicting evidence may be briefly pointed up. "Hard" facts must be included. Both must be *relevant* in order to be listed in the facts entry. It is impossible to tell what is relevant until the entire case is read, as the ultimate determination of the rights and liabilities of the parties may turn on something buried deep in the opinion.

Generally, the facts entry should not be longer than three to five *short* sentences.

It is often helpful to identify the role played by a party in a given context. For example, in a construction contract case the identification of a party as the "contractor" or "builder" alleviates the need to tell that that party was the one who was supposed to have built the house.

It is always helpful, and a good general practice, to identify the "plaintiff" and the "defendant." This may seem elementary and uncomplicated, but, especially in view of the creative editing practiced by some casebook editors, it is sometimes a difficult or even impossible task. Bear in mind that the *party presently* seeking something from this court may not be the plaintiff, and that sometimes only the cross-claim of a defendant is treated in the excerpt. Confusing or misaligning the parties can ruin your analysis and understanding of the case.

ISSUE: A statement of the general legal question answered by or illustrated in the case. For clarity, the issue is best put in the form of a question capable of a "yes" or "no" answer. In reality, the issue is simply the Rule of Law put in the form of a question (e.g., "May an offer be accepted by performance?").

The major problem presented in discerning what is *the* issue in the case is that an opinion usually purports to raise and answer several questions. However, except for rare cases, only one such question is really the issue in the case. Collateral issues not necessary to the resolution of the matter in controversy are handled by the court by language known as *"obiter dictum"* or merely *"dictum."* While dicta may be included later in the brief, they have no place under the issue heading.

To find the issue, ask *who wants what* and then go on to ask *why did that party succeed or fail in getting it.* Once this is determined, the "why" should be turned into a question.

The complexity of the issues in the cases will vary, but in all cases a single-sentence question should sum up the issue. *In a few cases,* there will be two, or even more rarely, three issues of equal importance to the resolution of the case. Each should be expressed in a single-sentence question.

Since many issues are resolved by a court in coming to a final disposition of a case, the casebook editor will reproduce the portion of the opinion containing the issue or issues most relevant to the area of law under scrutiny. A noted law professor gave this advice: "Close the book; look at the title on the cover." Chances are, if it is Property, you need not concern yourself with whether, for example, the federal government's treatment of the plaintiff's land really raises a federal question sufficient to support jurisdiction on this ground in federal court.

The same rule applies to chapter headings designating sub-areas within the subjects. They tip you off as to what the text is designed to teach. The cases are arranged in a casebook to show a progression or development of the law, so that the preceding cases may also help.

It is also most important to remember to *read the notes and questions* at the end of a case to determine what the editors wanted you to have gleaned from it.

HOLDING AND DECISION: This section should succinctly explain the rationale of the court in arriving at its decision. In capsulizing the "reasoning" of the court, it should always include an application of the general rule or rules of law to the specific facts of the case. Hidden justifications come to light in this entry; the reasons for the state of the law, the public policies, the biases and prejudices, those considerations that influence the justices' thinking and, ultimately, the outcome of the case. At the end, there should be a short indication of the disposition or procedural resolution of the case (e.g., "Decision of the trial court for Mr. Smith (P) reversed").

The foregoing format is designed to help you "digest" the reams of case material with which you will be faced in your law school career. Once mastered by practice, it will place at your fingertips the information the authors of your casebooks have sought to impart to you in case-by-case illustration and analysis.

B. Be as Economical as Possible in Briefing Cases

Once armed with a format that encourages succinctness, it is as important to be economical with regard to the time spent on the actual reading of the case as it is to be economical in the writing of the brief itself. This does not mean "skimming" a case. Rather, it means reading the case with an "eye" trained to recognize into which "section" of your brief a particular passage or line fits and having a system for quickly and precisely marking the case so that the passages fitting any one particular part of

the brief can be easily identified and brought together in a concise and accurate manner when the brief is actually written.

It is of no use to simply repeat everything in the opinion of the court; record only enough information to trigger your recollection of what the court said. Nevertheless, an accurate statement of the "law of the case," i.e., the legal principle applied to the facts, is absolutely essential to class preparation and to learning the law under the case method.

To that end, it is important to develop a "shorthand" that you can use to make margin notations. These notations will tell you at a glance in which section of the brief you will be placing that particular passage or portion of the opinion.

Some students prefer to underline all the salient portions of the opinion (with a pencil or colored underliner marker), making marginal notations as they go along. Others prefer the color-coded method of underlining, utilizing different colors of markers to underline the salient portions of the case, each separate color being used to represent a different section of the brief. For example, blue underlining could be used for passages relating to the rule of law, yellow for those relating to the issue, and green for those relating to the holding and decision, etc. While it has its advocates, the color-coded method can be confusing and time-consuming (all that time spent on changing colored markers). Furthermore, it can interfere with the continuity and concentration many students deem essential to the reading of a case for maximum comprehension. In the end, however, it is a matter of personal preference and style. Just remember, whatever method you use, underlining must be used sparingly or its value is lost.

If you take the marginal notation route, an efficient and easy method is to go along underlining the key portions of the case and placing in the margin alongside them the following "markers" to indicate where a particular passage or line "belongs" in the brief you will write:

N   (NATURE OF CASE)
RL   (RULE OF LAW)
I   (ISSUE)
HL   (HOLDING AND DECISION, relates to the RULE OF LAW behind the decision)
HR   (HOLDING AND DECISION, gives the RATIONALE or reasoning behind the decision)
HA   (HOLDING AND DECISION, APPLIES the general principle(s) of law to the facts of the case to arrive at the decision)

Remember that a particular passage may well contain information necessary to more than one part of your brief, in which case you simply note that in the margin. If you are using the color-coded underlining method instead of margin notation, simply make asterisks or checks in the margin next to the passage in question in the colors that indicate the additional sections of the brief where it might be utilized.

The economy of utilizing "shorthand" in marking cases for briefing can be maintained in the actual brief writing process itself by utilizing "law student shorthand" within the brief. There are many commonly used words and phrases for which abbreviations can be substituted in your briefs (and in your class notes also). You can develop abbreviations that are personal to you and which will save you a lot of time. A reference list of briefing abbreviations can be found on page xii of this book.

C. Use Both the Briefing Process and the Brief as a Learning Tool

Now that you have a format and the tools for briefing cases efficiently, the most important thing is to make the time spent in briefing profitable to you and to make the most advantageous use of the briefs you create. Of course, the briefs are invaluable for classroom reference when you are called upon to explain or analyze a particular case. However, they are also useful in reviewing for exams. A quick glance at the fact summary should bring the case to mind, and a rereading of the rule of law should enable you to go over the underlying legal concept in your mind, how it was applied in that particular case, and how it might apply in other factual settings.

As to the value to be derived from engaging in the briefing process itself, there is an immediate benefit that arises from being forced to sift through the essential facts and reasoning from the court's opinion and to succinctly express them in your own words in your brief. The process ensures that you understand the case and the point that it illustrates, and that means you will be ready to absorb further analysis and information brought forth in class. It also ensures you will have something to say when called upon in class. The briefing process helps develop a mental agility for getting to the *gist* of a case and for identifying, expounding on, and applying the legal concepts and issues found there. The briefing process is the mental process on which you must rely in taking law school examinations; it is also the mental process upon which a lawyer relies in serving his clients and in making his living.

acceptance	acp	offer	O
affirmed	aff	offeree	OE
answer	ans	offeror	OR
assumption of risk	a/r	ordinance	ord
attorney	atty	pain and suffering	p/s
beyond a reasonable doubt	b/r/d	parol evidence	p/e
bona fide purchaser	BFP	plaintiff	P
breach of contract	br/k	prima facie	p/f
cause of action	c/a	probable cause	p/c
common law	c/l	proximate cause	px/c
Constitution	Con	real property	r/p
constitutional	con	reasonable doubt	r/d
contract	K	reasonable man	r/m
contributory negligence	c/n	rebuttable presumption	rb/p
cross	x	remanded	rem
cross-complaint	x/c	res ipsa loquitur	RIL
cross-examination	x/ex	respondeat superior	r/s
cruel and unusual punishment	c/u/p	Restatement	RS
defendant	D	reversed	rev
dismissed	dis	Rule Against Perpetuities	RAP
double jeopardy	d/j	search and seizure	s/s
due process	d/p	search warrant	s/w
equal protection	e/p	self-defense	s/d
equity	eq	specific performance	s/p
evidence	ev	statute of limitations	S/L
exclude	exc	statute of frauds	S/F
exclusionary rule	exc/r	statute	S
felony	f/n	summary judgment	s/j
freedom of speech	f/s	tenancy in common	t/c
good faith	g/f	tenancy at will	t/w
habeas corpus	h/c	tenant	t
hearsay	hr	third party	TP
husband	H	third party beneficiary	TPB
in loco parentis	ILP	transferred intent	TI
injunction	inj	unconscionable	uncon
inter vivos	I/v	unconstitutional	unconst
joint tenancy	j/t	undue influence	u/e
judgment	judgt	Uniform Commercial Code	UCC
jurisdiction	jur	unilateral	uni
last clear chance	LCC	vendee	VE
long-arm statute	LAS	vendor	VR
majority view	maj	versus	v
meeting of minds	MOM	void for vagueness	VFV
minority view	min	weight of the evidence	w/e
Miranda warnings	Mir/w	weight of authority	w/a
Miranda rule	Mir/r	wife	W
negligence	neg	with	w/
notice	ntc	within	w/i
nuisance	nus	without prejudice	w/o/p
obligation	ob	without	w/o
obscene	obs	wrongful death	wr/d

Table of Cases

CHAPTER 1

An Overview of the Taxation of Corporations and Shareholders

Quick Reference Rules of Law

United Parcel Service of America, Inc. v. Commissioner

Corporate taxpayer (P) v. Government official (D)

254 F.3d 1014 (11th Cir. 2001).

NATURE OF THE CASE: Appeal from judgment imposing additional taxes and penalties for the tax year 1984.

FACT SUMMARY: United Parcel Service of America (UPS) (P) contended that certain restructuring had economic substance and a business purpose and was therefore not liable for additional taxes and penalties.

🏛 RULE OF LAW
If certain transactions result in tax benefits, the economic substance doctrine (sham transaction doctrine) will allow the company to receive those benefits \only if the transaction has economic effects and a business purpose. According to Frank Lyon Co. v. United States, 435 U.S. 561, 583–84 (1978), a company may receive tax benefits if there are genuine enforceable obligations by an unrelated party.

FACTS: UPS (P) is in the business of shipping packages. Around the time of this action, it was the policy of UPS (P) to reimburse customers up to $100 for lost or damaged packages. UPS customers were also given the option of paying $.25 per additional $100 for UPS (P) to process and pay claims on lost or damaged packages that exceeded $100 in value. This was called the excess value charge. UPS (P) always took great care in safeguarding and tracking packages from customers who paid the excess value charge, leading to very few claims paid by UPS, resulting in a large profit from the excess value charges. The excess value charges were reported and taxed as profit, and the claims paid on the lost or damaged packages were deducted as expenses. In 1983, UPS (P) was approached by its insurance broker, who suggested a way to reduce taxes on the profits from the excess value charges. According to the new plan, UPS (P) purchased an insurance policy through National Union Fire Insurance Company (NUF) and created an overseas affiliate, Overseas Partners, Ltd. (OPL), which entered into a reinsurance treaty with NUF. NUF collected premiums from the excess value payments, and premiums paid by NUF to OPL were equivalent to the excess value payments minus NUF's commissions and fees. UPS (P) then did not report the excess value payments as income, nor did it deduct claims paid as expenses. It did, however, deduct as expenses the fees and commissions to NUF. The IRS (D) claimed that the new plan had no economic substance or business purpose, and therefore the excess value payments should have been taxed as income.

ISSUE: Did the new plan have economic substance and business purpose, entitling it to tax relief?

HOLDING AND DECISION: (Cox, J.) Yes. The new plan by UPS did have economic substance and business

purpose that entitled it to certain tax benefits. In order for UPS to receive the tax benefits of the new plan, the plan must have economic effects aside from the tax benefits. This determination of economic effects rests on whether there are enforceable obligations against unrelated parties. First, as an insurance company, NUF assumed a real risk, which was liability for UPS customers' lost or damaged packages. Second, OPL was an independent entity, separate from UPS. The money UPS received from the excess value charges could not be used for any other purpose (for example, salaries, investments, or capital improvement) other than premiums to NUF. Third, although NUF had a reinsurance treaty with OPL, that is not an absolute guarantee that OPL will not default. Therefore, this plan had real economic effects and was not per se a sham transaction. In addition to economic effects, there must also be a business purpose, and there was a business purpose in this case. In determining whether a business purpose exists, all that is required is that the plan figures in with a profit-seeking, bona fide business. Tax planning is part of a profit-seeking bona fide business, and the mere fact that tax benefits motivate the transaction does not negate the business purpose. Therefore, since the new plan by UPS had economic effects and a business purpose, it should receive the tax benefits. Reversed and remanded.

DISSENT: (Ryskamp, J.) This was a sham transaction. OPL was not a legitimate insurance company, and there were no real obligations placed on NUF. UPS paid NUF commissions and fees to do nothing, and the risk of loss to NUF was "infinitesimal." UPS continued to collect the excess value charges and to pay the claims the way it did before the new plan.

▶ ANALYSIS

It appears that it was unnecessary to address the issue of "business purpose," since the court used the tax benefits as the business purpose. This is not in line with *Kirchman v. Commissioner*, 862 F.2d 1486, 1492 (11th Cir. 1991) (see dissent) where a business will not receive tax benefits if there are no economic effects *other than tax benefits.* (Emphasis added.)

Quicknotes

REINSURANCE A contract between an insurer and a third party to insure the insurer against potential loss or liability resulting from a previous insurance contract.

Commissioner v. Bollinger

Government official (D) v. Shareholder (P)

485 U.S. 340 (1988).

NATURE OF CASE: Appeal of order invalidating a deficiency assessment.

FACT SUMMARY: The Internal Revenue Service (IRS) (D) contended that a corporation owned by Bollinger (P) could not be an agent of Bollinger (P) for tax purposes.

🏛 RULE OF LAW

For tax purposes, a corporation may be an agent of its shareholders.

FACTS: To avoid the application of Kentucky's usury laws, Bollinger (P), who wished to purchase certain real estate in partnership with various individuals, formed a corporation. The partners were the only shareholders. The corporation held title to the real estate after it was purchased. It was the understanding of all parties that the corporation would hold bare legal title as agent for the partnership. The property generated losses for several years, which the various partners deducted. The IRS (D) disallowed the deduction, stating that the losses belonged to the corporation. Bollinger (P) challenged this in Tax Court, which ruled in his favor. The court of appeals affirmed. The IRS (D) petitioned for certiorari.

ISSUE: For tax purposes, may a corporation be an agent of its shareholders?

HOLDING AND DECISION: (Scalia, J.) Yes. For tax purposes, a corporation may be an agent of its shareholders. Gain or loss in the use of property is generally realized by the owner thereof. However, if a corporation holds property as agent for a partnership, then for tax purposes the partnership is the owner. However, this Court has held that the corporation must be a truly separate entity for this to occur, as the potential for abuse would otherwise be too great. The IRS (D) takes this to mean that there cannot be ownership of the corporation by the partnership or its partners. The Court does not agree. It is of the opinion that if the corporation serves a legitimate business purpose apart from tax avoidance consequences, the separateness element will be met. The Court is satisfied that if a corporation acts as an agent for a certain asset for all purposes, and this is clearly manifested by a writing, no danger for abusive avoidance schemes exists. As this was the case here, the agency was valid. Affirmed.

▶ ANALYSIS

The seminal case in this area was *National Carbide Corp. v. Commissioner*, 336 U.S. 422 (1949). This was the Court's first major decision regarding the validity of corporate agency for tax purposes. The Court there decided that the corporate agent must have a business purpose apart from mere tax avoidance.

■══■

Quicknotes

CERTIORARI A discretionary writ issued by a superior court to an inferior court in order to review the lower court's decisions; the Supreme Court's writ ordering such review.

CORPORATION A distinct legal entity characterized by continuous existence; free alienability of interests held therein; centralized management; and limited liability on the part of the shareholders of the corporation.

SHAREHOLDER An individual who owns shares of stock in a corporation.

■══■

Formation of a Corporation

Quick Reference Rules of Law

Intermountain Lumber Co. v. Commissioner

Corporate taxpayer (P) v. Government official (D)

U.S. Tax Ct., 65 T.C. 1025 (1976).

NATURE OF CASE: Petition to determine taxability of transfer of assets to newly formed corporation.

FACT SUMMARY: After Shook transferred a sawmill to a new corporation, S&W, in exchange for most of its common stock, half of which he agreed to sell to Wilson, Intermountain Lumber (Intermountain) (P) acquired S&W, and in order for it to take a high, fair market basis in these assets for depreciation purposes it characterized Shook's transfer as a taxable sale.

🏛 RULE OF LAW
If an individual or group of individuals forms a corporation by transferring property in exchange for at least 80% of the voting stock and at least 80% of all other classes of stock, then that transfer of assets is tax-free under IRC § 351.

FACTS: Shook owned a sawmill that Wilson used to process logs into finished lumber. When the sawmill needed replacing, Shook turned to Wilson to co-guarantee a $200,000 loan. Shook, Wilson, and two others then incorporated the sawmill business as S&W, Inc., and Shook transferred the sawmill to S&W in exchange for 364 shares of S&W common stock. In exchange for Wilson's help with the loan, Shook agreed to sell Wilson half of his S&W shares at $500 per, plus interest, to be paid in installments; for each principal payment, a transfer of Shook's shares to Wilson on the corporate record would be shown. Three years later, all S&W stock was bought out by Intermountain (P). Intermountain (P) wanted the S&W incorporation exchange treated as a taxable sale so that it could take advantage of the new fair market value basis for depreciation; the Internal Revenue Service (IRS) (D) argued the transfer of assets to S&W was a tax-free exchange under IRC § 351.

ISSUE: Is the transfer of assets in exchange for stock for the purpose of incorporation treated as a tax-free exchange under Internal Revenue Code (IRC) § 351, if the transferor has "immediate control" of over 80% of voting and non-voting stock after the transfer?

HOLDING AND DECISION: (Wiles, J.) Yes. IRC § 351 provides that no gain shall be recognized if property is transferred to a corporation by one or more persons solely in exchange for stock and if the transferors after the exchange control the corporation. "Control" is defined by § 368(c) as ownership of at least 80% of the voting power of stocks entitled to vote and at least 80% of the total number of shares of all other classes of stock. In this case, Shook transferred the sawmill to S&W. Under his agreement with Wilson, Shook irrevocably relinquished his legal right to determine whether to keep the shares he contracted to sell to Wilson; he was obliged to transfer the stock as he received Wilson's payments. This sale was an integral part of the incorporation transaction. All evidence—Wilson's right to prepay principal, the parties' characterization of the agreement as a sale, Wilson's deduction of interest expenses—indicate the parties intended a final sale, not an "option" agreement as contended by the IRS. Thus, the transfer by Shook to S&W was a taxable sale and IRC § 351 does not apply. Held for petitioner.

▶ ANALYSIS

"Property" transferable to a new corporation includes cash, capital, inventory, accounts receivable, intellectual property, and licenses. IRC § 351(d)(1), however, specifically excludes services from the definition of "property"; although an incorporator who provides only services will not be considered part of the "control" group for purposes of the § 351 tax-free exchange, one who provides both services and property in exchange for stock will have all of his shares included in the 80% figure.

■=■

Peracchi v. Commissioner

Shareholder (P) v. Government official (D)

143 F.3d 487 (9th Cir. 1998).

NATURE OF CASE: Appeal from Tax Court ruling upholding tax.

FACT SUMMARY: Peracchi (P) claimed that a promissory note he gave to his corporation was not an unenforceable gift that would trigger tax liability.

🏛 RULE OF LAW
Promissory notes from individuals to their closely held corporations may be used to offset gains from transferring property encumbered by debt.

FACTS: Peracchi (P) contributed two parcels of real estate to his closely held corporation, NAC. The property had liabilities that exceeded Peracchi's (P) basis by half a million dollars. To avoid having to recognize a taxable gain from this transaction, Peracchi (P) also executed a promissory note in favor of NAC for a million dollars at 11% interest over ten years. The Internal Revenue Service (IRS) (D) claimed that his note wasn't true indebtedness because Peracchi (P) could choose not to have NAC repay it. The IRS (D) maintained that it should be treated as an unenforceable gift and that Peracchi (P) must recognize a taxable gain from giving NAC the debt-encumbered property. The Tax Court agreed with the IRS (D), and Peracchi (P) appealed.

ISSUE: May promissory notes from individuals to their closely held corporations be used to offset taxable gains when property encumbered with debt is also transferred?

HOLDING AND DECISION: (Kozinski, J.) Yes. Promissory notes from individuals to their closely held corporations may be used to offset gains from transferring property encumbered by debt. Ordinarily, shareholders contributing capital to their corporation can do so without recognizing a gain. This nonrecognition assumes that the contribution amounts to nothing more than a nominal change in the form of ownership. The central exception to this rule is when an individual receives money or property other than stock in exchange for the capital or property contributed. In cases where property encumbered by liabilities is transferred to the corporation, § 357(a) of the Tax Code allows taxpayers to avoid treating the assumption of liability as an immediately taxable event, so long as there isn't a negative basis in the property. Thus, in the present case, Peracchi's (P) contribution of debt-encumbered property would have triggered tax consequences except for the fact that the promissory note removed the negative basis. Still, the IRS (D) maintained that the note was merely a paper promise that was not entitled to legal significance. However, this view ignores the fact that Peracchi (P) would be personally liable for the note if NAC were to go bankrupt. The real possibility of increased personal loss shows that this is genuine indebtedness and that Peracchi (P) is entitled to a step-up basis for this contribution. Accordingly, Peracchi (P) should not have been taxed on any gain for transferring the property to NAC. Reversed and remanded.

DISSENT: (Fernandez, J.) Allowing taxpayers to use unsecured promissory notes to their corporations to avoid the tax consequences of getting rid of debt-encumbered property simply creates basis without any cost to the taxpayer.

▶ ANALYSIS

The majority acknowledged the possibility that it was approving a new type of tax shelter. However, it was more convinced that Peracchi's (P) increased debt exposure through the note significantly protected against that possibility. In any event, it does seem that Peracchi (P), through NAC, may not ever enforce the note against himself.

Quicknotes

PROMISSORY NOTE A written promise to tender a stated amount of money at a designated time and to a designated person.

Hempt Brothers, Inc. v. United States

Corporate taxpayer (P) v. Federal government (D)

490 F.2d 1172; *cert. denied*, 419 U.S. 826 (1974).

NATURE OF CASE: Appeal from tax deficiency assessment.

FACT SUMMARY: Hempt (P) contended the receivables it acquired were not property under IRC § 351, and thus the principles of the taxation under that section were inapplicable.

🏛 RULE OF LAW
Accounts receivable are property under Internal Revenue Code (IRC) § 352, yet a transfer of such for stock is not a taxable transaction.

FACTS: Hempt (P), a cash method partnership, transferred zero basis accounts receivable to a newly formed corporation in exchange for all the corporation's stock. The Commissioner (D) contended the zero basis carried over to the corporation which must pay tax upon collection. Hempt (P), to take advantage of the statute of limitations on past years, argued the receivables were not property, § 351 did not apply, and the partnership should bear the tax burden. The district court held the receivables were property and that the corporation should be taxed. Hempt (P) appealed.

ISSUE: Are accounts receivables property under IRC § 352, and transfer of such therefore constitutes a taxable transaction?

HOLDING AND DECISION: (Aldisert, J.) Yes. Accounts receivables are property under IRC § 352, and a transfer of such for stock is not a taxable transaction. The receivables are a present right to future payment. Thus, they fall into the classic definition of property under IRC § 352. Even though this may conflict with the assignment of income doctrine which taxes the transfer of assigned income, this does not generate a taxable transaction. IRC § 352 is a specific congressional pronouncement that incorporations are to be encouraged and facilitated. An alternative holding would frustrate this intent. Affirmed.

▌ *ANALYSIS*

In this case, the court was faced with conflicting tax doctrines requiring one to be subordinated to the other. When property is transferred to a newly formed corporation, it is not taxed as it is considered a reorganization under IRC § 351. The court felt the facilitation of incorporating was more important than the realization of a taxable event and, thus, held § 357 superior to the assignment of income doctrine.

Quicknotes

ACCOUNTS RECEIVABLE Amounts that are owed pursuant to an open account and that arise in the normal course of business dealings.

STATUTE OF LIMITATIONS A law prescribing the period in which a legal action may be commenced.

Black & Decker Corp. v. United States

Corporate taxpayer (P) v. Federal government (D)

436 F.3d 431 (4th Cir. 2006).

NATURE OF CASE: Appeal from grant of summary judgment to taxpayer and denial of summary judgment to the Internal Revenue Service in action for refund of federal taxes.

FACT SUMMARY: Black & Decker Corp. (B & D) (P) created Black & Decker Health Management, Inc. (BDHMI), transferring $561 million in cash in exchange for preferred stock worth $1 million and BDHMI's assumption of contingent employee and retiree healthcare benefits, worth $560 million. B & D (P) then sold the stock for $1 million and claimed a $560 million capital loss on the sale and brought suit for a refund, contending that its basis in the BDHMI stock was $561 million. The Internal Revenue Service (IRS) (D) contended that B & D's (P) basis was only $1 million. The trial court granted summary judgment to B & D (P) and denied summary judgment to the IRS (D). The IRS (D) appealed, claiming the trial court's rulings were erroneous.

RULE OF LAW

(1) A transferor taxpayer in an Internal Revenue Code (IRC) § 351 exchange may benefit from the exception provided in IRC § 357(c)(3)(A) where contingent liabilities transferred to the transferee would give rise to a deduction, so that the assumed contingent liabilities are not treated as "money received" under IRC § 358 and do not reduce the basis of the stock received by the transferor in the exchange.

(2) To determine if a transaction falls under the sham transaction doctrine, it must be determined whether there is a reasonable chance the taxpayer may profit from the transaction apart from its tax benefits.

FACTS: B & D (P) sold three of its businesses in one year and generated significant capital gains. That same year, B & D (P) created BDHMI. B & D (P) transferred approximately $561 million in cash to BDHMI along with $560 million in contingent employee healthcare claims in exchange for newly issued preferred stock in BDHMI. B & D (P) sold its stock in BDHMI to an independent third party for $1 million. B & D (P) asserted that it had created BDHMI to outsource employee and retiree medical claims to control costs. It also asserted that its basis in the BDHMI stock was $561 million and claimed a $560 million capital loss on the sale, which it reported on its federal tax return. B & D (P) applied a portion of the capital loss to offset its capital gains from selling the three businesses, and carried back and forward the remaining capital loss to offset gains in prior and future tax years. B & D (P) brought suit for a refund of federal taxes, relying on Revenue Ruling 95-74 for its position, contending that it was not required to reduce its stock basis by the "contingent" liabilities assumed by BDHMI because they were not "liabilities" for purposes of IRC §§ 357(c)(1) and 358(d). The IRS (D) argued that B & D's (P) stock basis equaled the $561 million cash transferred less the $560 million liabilities assumed, i.e., $1 million, so that there was no loss on the sale. The IRS (D) moved for summary judgment, as did B & D (P). The district court found that the BDHMI had been constituted for a valid business purpose so that all of its transactions were "objectively reasonable" and could not be disregarded for tax purposes. Accordingly, it granted summary judgment to B & D (P) while denying the IRS's summary judgment motion. The IRS (D) appealed and the court of appeals granted review.

ISSUE:

(1) May a transferor taxpayer in an IRC § 351 exchange benefit from the exception provided in IRC § 357(c)(3)(A) where contingent liabilities transferred to the transferee would give rise to a deduction, so that the assumed contingent liabilities are not treated as "money received" under IRC § 358 and do not reduce the basis of the stock received by the transferor in the exchange?

(2) To determine if a transaction falls under the sham transaction doctrine, must it be determined whether there is a reasonable chance the taxpayer may profit from the transaction apart from its tax benefits?

HOLDING AND DECISION: (Michael, J.)

(1) Yes. A transferor taxpayer in an IRC § 351 exchange may benefit from the exception provided in IRC § 357(c)(3)(A) where contingent liabilities transferred to the transferee would give rise to a deduction, so that the assumed contingent liabilities are not treated as "money received" under IRC § 358 and do not reduce the basis of the stock received by the transferor in the exchange. The statutory framework governing the exchange at issue is as follows. First, IRC § 351 is implicated here because IRC § 351(a) provides that no gain or loss is recognized if property is transferred to a corporation by one or more persons solely in exchange for voting stock in the transferee corporation, and immediately after the exchange the transferor is in control of the transferee. Here, B & D (P) has transferred money to BDHMI for preferred stock and after the exchange controls BDHMI. However, the transfer does not fall squarely within IRC § 351(a) because the transfer was not "solely" for voting stock, but was also made for the assumption of contingent liabilities. The transaction can nonetheless be tax-free to B & D (P) if it can shown that the provisions of

Continued on next page.

IRC § 357(a) are satisfied. IRC § 357(a) provides that transactions are treated as IRC § 351(a) tax-free transactions if they would satisfy IRC § 351(a) but for the fact that the transferee, in consideration for the transferor's property, not only gave its stock but also assumed the transferor's liability. In such cases, IRC § 357(a) prevents the transferee's assumption of liability from being treated as taxable money or property received by the transferor—unless the principal purpose of the transaction is to avoid paying federal tax. In addition to the issue of whether the transaction is tax-free is the concept of basis computation, which requires a determination of whether there was a capital gain or loss as governed by IRC § 358. Under IRC § 358(a)(1), an IRC § 351 transferor's basis in the stock received from the transferee is the same as the basis of the property the transferor surrendered, reduced by the amount of any "money received." As here, contingent liabilities assumed by the transferee are treated as "money received," which reduces basis unless the liability assumed is one that would be excluded under IRC § 357(c)(3). That section excludes from basis reduction any "liability the payment of which . . . would give rise to a deduction." Therefore, to prevail on summary judgment, the IRS (D) must show that as a matter of law B & D (P) was not entitled to the exception provided under IRC § 357(c)(3). The Internal Revenue Code is subject to the same rules of statutory construction that any statute is subject to. One of the principles of statutory construction is that a court will give effect to a statute's plain meaning. Applying this principle here, it is clear that the contingent liabilities transferred to BDHMI would fall within the IRC § 357(c)(3) exception if they were deductible. However, the statute does not clearly indicate whether the deduction can be taken by the transferee or the transferor. Therefore, the legislative history must be looked to for clarification. The legislative history indicates that the deduction was to be taken by the transferor. Therefore, the contingent liabilities fall with the IRC § 357(c)(3) exception, and under IRC § 358, they are not treated as money received, so do not reduce B & D's (P) basis in the stock it received in the exchange. Accordingly, the district court was correct in denying summary judgment to the IRS (D). Affirmed as to this issue.

(2) Yes. To determine if a transaction falls under the sham transaction doctrine, it must be determined whether there is a reasonable chance the taxpayer may profit from the transaction apart from its tax benefits. The IRS (D) puts forth two arguments as to why summary judgment for B & D (P) was inappropriate. The first is statutory, under which the IRS (D) attempts to connect the purpose of IRC § 357(b)—to render assumed liabilities as "money received" where the taxpayer's principal purpose in transferring liability is to avoid federal income tax on the IRC § 351 exchange—to IRC § 358's basis computation rules. This attempted connection is rejected as unsupported. The next argument is based on the judge-made sham transaction doctrine, which provides that a transaction that literally complies with the terms of the IRC but that is devoid of any legitimate business purpose may be disregarded. The test for whether a transaction fits within the sham transaction doctrine has two parts. The first requires a finding that the taxpayer was motivated by no business purposes other than obtaining tax benefits in entering the transaction. This is a subjective test. The second requires a finding that the transaction has no economic substance because no reasonable possibility of a profit exists. This is an objective test. Here, B & D (P) conceded the subjective prong of the test by conceding that it entered the transaction only for tax avoidance reasons. However, the district court incorrectly applied the objective prong of the test. Instead of inquiring into whether there was a reasonable possibility of profit from the particular transaction at issue apart from its tax benefits, the court ruled that a corporation and its transactions are objectively reasonable, despite any tax-avoidance motive, so long as the corporation engages in bona fide economically based business transactions. This mischaracterizes the objective test, which focuses not on the general business activities of a corporation, but on the specific transaction whose tax consequences are in dispute. Because the district court applied the wrong test, the undisputed facts on which it relied in granting summary judgment to B & D (P) are irrelevant so that summary judgment should not have issued for B & D (P). Moreover, B & D's (P) argument that the district court's objective test was correct because BDHMI's corporate identity was not a sham is rejected. That is because the IRS (D) is not arguing here that BDHMI's corporate identity separate from B & D (P) must be disregarded for tax purposes, such that income earned by one is to be attributed to the other; a parent corporation's transaction with a subsidiary corporation may be a sham under the objective prong even if the subsidiary is entitled to regard its income as distinct from the parents because the subsidiary is not itself a sham. The objective prong of the sham transaction test focuses on reasonable expected profits from a transaction; it does not focus, as the district court did, on the transaction's "real economic effects." Applying this test, it is clear that here the IRS (D) adduced ample evidence for a reasonable trier of fact to find that there could be no profit in the transaction apart from its tax benefits. Accordingly, the facts to be determined under this test are in dispute and a triable issue has been created; the issue must go to trial. Reversed as to this issue.

▶ ANALYSIS

Contingent liability shelters of the type presented by this case are now largely blocked by IRC § 358(h), which Congress enacted as part of the Community Renewal Tax Relief Act of

Continued on next page.

2000. P.L. 106-554, § 1(a)(7), 114 Stat. 2763 (2000) and which was neither in effect for the tax year involved (1998) nor applies retroactively. Section 358(h) provides that, in a transfer such as the one in this case, if the transferor's basis exceeds the fair market value of the stock received, the transferor must reduce that basis by the amount of any "liability" assumed by the transferee (or another person) as part of the exchange. This would cover those situations where the assumed liability is contingent or excluded under § 357(c)(3). In addition, in 2001 the IRS issued Notice 2001-17 on contingent liability tax shelters, which put corporations on notice that the IRS would challenge transactions of the type at issue here.

Quicknotes

SUMMARY JUDGMENT Judgment rendered by a court in response to a motion made by one of the parties, claiming that the lack of a question of material fact in respect to an issue warrants disposition of the issue without consideration by the jury.

Commissioner v. Fink

Government official (D) v. Shareholder (P)

483 U.S. 89 (1987).

NATURE OF CASE: Appeal from reversal of denial of tax deduction.

FACT SUMMARY: The Finks (P) attempted to deduct the basis in shares they had surrendered to a corporation in which they retained control.

RULE OF LAW
A shareholder may not deduct the basis in shares he surrenders to a corporation in which he retains control.

FACTS: The Finks (P) owned 72.5% of Travco Corp. In an effort to make Travco more appealing to outside investors, the Finks (P) voluntarily surrendered 80,000 shares, reducing their control to 68.5%. The Finks (P) claimed the value of the shares as a loss on ordinary income. The Internal Revenue Service (IRS) (D) disallowed the deduction. The Tax Court agreed with the IRS (D), but the court of appeals reversed. The IRS (D) petitioned for certiorari.

ISSUE: May a shareholder deduct the basis in shares he surrenders to a corporation in which he retains control?

HOLDING AND DECISION: (Powell, J.) No. A shareholder may not deduct the basis in shares he surrenders to a corporation in which he retains control. It has long been the rule that capital contributions to a corporation are not deductible, as they are done for the benefit of the corporation, thus enhancing the value of the contributing shareholder's investment. The surrender of shares to a corporation is a very similar transaction, as it increases the value of the remaining shares. This alone argues strongly against allowing a deduction. In addition, if deductions were allowed, taxpayers could convert a capital loss treatment of a failing corporation into ordinary loss by surrendering shares immediately before insolvency. For these reasons, deductions of surrendered shares may not be allowed if the taxpayer continues to control the corporation. Reversed.

CONCURRENCE: (White, J.) There is no reason for not extending the rule to surrenders where the taxpayer does not retain control.

CONCURRENCE: (Scalia, J.) The capital contribution analogy is inappropriate. Nonetheless the purpose was to improve the corporation, and the rule announced here was proper.

ANALYSIS

The issue presented here was first ruled upon in 1941 in *Miller v. Commissioner*, 45 B.T.A. 292. For several decades thereafter, this rule was generally followed. In the 1980s, courts of appeal began to hold to the contrary, culminating in the present decision.

Quicknotes

CERTIORARI A discretionary writ issued by a superior court to an inferior court in order to review the lower court's decisions; the Supreme Court's writ ordering such review.

CORPORATION A distinct legal entity characterized by continuous existence; free alienability of interests held therein; centralized management; and limited liability on the part of the shareholders of the corporation.

SHAREHOLDER An individual who owns shares of stock in a corporation.

CHAPTER 3

The Capital Structure of a Corporation

Quick Reference Rules of Law

Fin Hay Realty Co. v. United States

Corporate taxpayer (P) v. Federal government (D)

398 F.2d 694 (3d Cir. 1968).

NATURE OF CASE: Appeal from denial of tax refund.

FACT SUMMARY: The Commissioner (D) contended payments made by a close corporation to its shareholders were not in retirement of debt and therefore were taxable.

🏛 RULE OF LAW
The taxpayer has the burden of showing that distributions from a close corporation are in retirement of debt where such are challenged as capital distributions.

FACTS: Finlaw and Hay formed Fin Hay Realty Co. (P) and were its sole shareholders. They individually made loans to the corporation. The loans were paid off in installments over many years. Although all formalities of the transactions indicated they were loans, the Commissioner (D) contended the disbursements were capital distributions and not debt payments, thus rendering them taxable. The district court held the payments were capital distributions, and Fin Hay (P) appealed.

ISSUE: Does the taxpayer have the burden of showing that distributions from a close corporation are debt retirement payments when they are challenged as capital distributions?

HOLDING AND DECISION: (Freedman, J.) Yes. The taxpayer has the burden of showing that distributions from a close corporation are in retirement of debt where such are challenged as capital distributions. While all formalities of debt were met in this case, the court must look to the substance of the transactions. The purported lenders were the sole shareholders in the corporation. Each "loan" was made in an identical amount by each shareholder. No change in equity position could be made. Further, although the notes were demand notes, they could not be repaid for several years. Only a controlling shareholder would make such an investment. Thus, the notes cannot be considered debts of the corporation, and its payments thereon were not deductible as interest. Affirmed.

▶ ANALYSIS

Whether an instrument is to be considered debt as opposed to a stock interest depends upon the resolution of several factual issues. The courts often consider the following elements in making this determination: (1) the party's intent; (2) the form of the investment; and (3) the extent of participation in management by the holder. These elements are neither exhaustive nor dispositive of the issue which has proved nebulous to a majority of courts.

CHAPTER 4

Nonliquidating Distributions

Quick Reference Rules of Law

Nicholls, North, Buse Co. v. Commissioner

Corporate taxpayer (P) v. Government official (D)

U.S. Tax Ct., 56 T.C. 1225 (1971).

NATURE OF CASE: Challenge to notice of deficiency.

FACT SUMMARY: The Internal Revenue Service (IRS) (D) contended that personal use of a yacht owned by Nicholls, North (P) constituted a constructive dividend.

🏛 RULE OF LAW
Corporate expenditures for the personal benefit of stockholders, or the availability of corporate-owned facilities to stockholders for their personal benefit, may be classified as constructive dividends.

FACTS: Herbert and Charlotte Resenhoeft (P) and their two sons owned all of the shares in Nicholls, North, Buse Co. (P). Nicholls (P) bought a fifty-two-foot yacht at a total cost of $68,290 and passed a resolution that Herbert (P) was responsible for expenses due to personal use of the boat. Subsequently, Herbert's (P) son used the yacht for personal reasons. The IRS (D) claimed that Herbert (P) could be taxed on the purchase price for the yacht or on a dividend equal to its fair rental value. Herbert (P) contended that he agreed to the acquisition of the yacht to benefit the corporation only and therefore his son's personal use of the yacht should not be attributed to him.

ISSUE: May corporate expenditures for the personal benefit of stockholders, or the availability of corporate-owned facilities to stockholders for their personal benefit, be classified as constructive dividends?

HOLDING AND DECISION: [Judge not stated in casebook excerpt.] Yes. Corporate expenditures for the personal benefit of stockholders, or the availability of corporate-owned facilities to stockholders for their personal benefit, may be classified as constructive dividends. In this case, the Nicholls (P) yacht was used for business purposes 25% of the time and for personal purposes 75% of the time. The use of the yacht by James—a shareholder in his own right—may be imputed to his father, Herbert, (P), who was in control of Nicholls (P). Since Herbert (P) made the decision to have Nicholls (P) purchase the yacht and then permitted his sons to use it as they wished, the constructive dividend must be attributed to Herbert (P). However, since Nicholls (P) clearly owns the yacht, Herbert (P) has not received a dividend equivalent to the yacht's cost. Instead, the fair rental value of the yacht for the period of its use in 1964 should be the measure of the dividend received. Herbert Resenhoeft (P) gained personal benefit from the yacht and therefore received a constructive dividend equal to 75% of that amount.

▶ ANALYSIS

Corporations often try to circumvent the nondeductible nature of dividends by concealing them as salaries and loans to shareholders or as interest on shareholder debt. Another popular device is the "bargain sale," whereby corporate property is purchased by a shareholder for substantially less than an arm's length price. Under those circumstances, the IRS will increase both the income of the property's seller and the basis of the property to reflect the true arm's length price.

Quicknotes

CONSTRUCTIVE DIVIDEND A benefit made by a corporation to a shareholder that is taxable even though the benefit was not designated as a dividend.

TSN Liquidating Corp. v. United States

Corporate taxpayer (P) v. Federal government (D)

624 F.2d 1328 (5th Cir. 1980).

NATURE OF CASE: Appeal from denial of tax refund.

FACT SUMMARY: The district court held that assets distributed to TSN Corp. (P) by its subsidiary, CLIC, just prior to TSN's (P) sale of all the capital stock of CLIC, constituted part of the consideration for such sale rather than a dividend.

🏛 RULE OF LAW
Assets removed from a corporation in contemplation of sale of the stock of the corporation, when retained in good faith by the sellers, are dividends.

FACTS: TSN (P) sold all its capital stock in its subsidiary for a sum of cash. Just prior to the sale, stocks held by CLIC, the subsidiary, were distributed as a dividend in kind to TSN (P) shareholders. They were claimed as dividends for tax purposes, yet the district court in a refund suit held they were part of the consideration given in the sale. TSN (P) appealed.

ISSUE: Are assets removed from a subsidiary to a parent in anticipation of the parent's divestiture of the subsidiary stock treated as dividends?

HOLDING AND DECISION: (Randall, J.) Yes. Assets removed from a corporation in contemplation of a sale of the stock of the corporation, when retained in good faith by the sellers, are dividends. They are not considered part of the price paid for the stock, as in economic reality, no sale occurred. The sellers merely retained that which they did not wish to sell. Thus, the transfer is taxed as a dividend. Reversed and remanded.

▌*ANALYSIS*

In order for the distribution of assets to qualify as a dividend, not only must the sellers retain the distribution, but must do so in a good faith attempt to ensure the assets will not be transferred to the buyer. If they are, clearly they would be considered part of the purchase price and not dividends. The court here relies on the basic tenet of tax law that the tax incidence must fall based upon the substance, rather than the form, of the transaction. Since this case was decided, several provisions of the IRC have come into play when determining whether a pre-sale distribution, such as occurred here, is viable. First, Internal Revenue Code (IRC) § 301(e) may reduce the benefit of such a transaction by requiring that, in the case of a 20% or greater shareholder, and for the purpose of determining taxable dividend income, the distributing corporation's earnings and profits must be determined without regard to the adjustments provided in §§ 312(k) and 312(n). One also has to consider that such a distribution may adjust a shareholder's basis in the stock downward as a result of the pre-sale dividend.

∎═∎

Quicknotes

ASSET An item of real or personal property that is owned and has tangible value.

CAPITAL STOCK Total shares a corporation may issue according to the corporation's articles of incorporation; includes both common and preferred stock.

DIVIDEND The payment of earnings to a corporation's shareholders in proportion to the amount of shares held.

GOOD FAITH An honest intention to abstain from taking advantage of another.

∎═∎

CHAPTER 5

Redemptions and Partial Liquidations

Quick Reference Rules of Law

Lynch v. Commissioner

Stockholder (P) v. Government official (D)

801 F.2d 1176 (9th Cir. 1986).

NATURE OF CASE: Appeal from denial of tax deficiency assessment.

FACT SUMMARY: The Tax Court held that the redemption of Lynch's (P) stock was a sale or exchange subject to capital gains treatment.

🏛 RULE OF LAW
A taxpayer who provides post-redemption services holds a prohibited interest in the corporation requiring the treatment of the redemption as a dividend distribution.

FACTS: Lynch (P) was the controlling shareholder in W.M. Lynch Co., a corporation. He sold his controlling share to his son, who then caused the corporation to redeem Lynch's (P) remaining shares. The corporation then contracted with Lynch (P) to pay him for consulting services. Lynch (P) treated the redemption as a long-term capital gain, and such was upheld by the Tax Court. The Commissioner (D) appealed, contending the consulting agreement constituted a prohibited interest in the corporation, requiring the redemption be treated as a dividend.

ISSUE: Does a taxpayer who provides post-redemption services hold a prohibited interest in the corporation?

HOLDING AND DECISION: (Hall, J.) Yes. A taxpayer who provides post-redemption services holds a prohibited interest in the corporation, requiring the redemption be treated as a dividend distribution. The taxpayer is not a creditor of the corporation following the redemption. The consulting services go to the essence of the corporation and thus allow for the exercise of control over corporate action. Therefore, the redemption was a dividend taxed as ordinary income. Reversed.

▶ ANALYSIS

The court noted its decision in this case was contradictory to *Estate of Lennard v. Commissioner*, 61 T.C. 554 (1974). In that case, a post-redemption stockholder acting as an independent contractor, as opposed to an employee, held no prohibited interest. The court here held the designation of independent contractor or employee was irrelevant. The crucial inquiry is whether management control or a financial interest is retained.

■■■■

United States v. Davis

Federal government (D) v. Shareholder (P)

397 U.S. 301; *rehearing denied*, 397 U.S. 1071 (1970).

NATURE OF CASE: Action for a refund of taxes paid.

FACT SUMMARY: Davis (P) purchased $25,000 worth of preferred stock in a corporation so that it could get a loan. When the loan was repaid, the corporation redeemed the stock and Davis (P) received $25,000. By that time, Davis (P) owned all of the corporation's common stock.

🏛 RULE OF LAW
In order for a redemption to be "not essentially equivalent to a dividend" under § 302(b)(1), a redemption must result in a meaningful reduction of the shareholder's interest in the corporation, and the existence of a bona fide business purpose is irrelevant in determining dividend equivalency.

FACTS: Davis (P), who owned common stock in a closely held corporation, purchased $25,000 worth of preferred stock to enable the corporation to obtain a loan. It was understood that the preferred stock would be redeemed after the loan was repaid. In the meantime, Davis (P) acquired all of the corporation's common stock. When the preferred stock was redeemed, Davis (P) reported the redemption as a capital gains transaction. The Commissioner claims the redemption was essentially equivalent to a dividend and thus should be taxed as ordinary income.

ISSUE: Where a corporation's sole owner causes part of his shares to be redeemed by the corporation, is the redemption essentially equivalent to a dividend even though there is a bona fide business purpose for the transaction?

HOLDING AND DECISION: (Marshall, J.) Yes. Section 302(b)(1) permits a redemption of stock to be treated as a capital gain rather than ordinary income if such redemption is "not essentially equivalent to a dividend." To satisfy the requirement of this section, a redemption must result in a meaningful reduction of the shareholder's interest in the corporation. Hence, a taxpayer such as Davis (P) who is the sole shareholder of a corporation both before and after a redemption of his preferred stock does not qualify under this test. It is true that in the past courts have held redemptions not to be dividends where there is a bona fide business purpose for the transaction. However, whether or not such a purpose exists is irrelevant in determining dividend equivalency. Reversed and remanded.

DISSENT: (Douglas, J.) The redemption was "not essentially equivalent to a dividend," since the bona fide business purpose of the redemption belied the payment of a dividend.

▶ ANALYSIS

In interpreting the "meaningful reduction" standard established by this case, the Internal Revenue Service has considered several factors, including the effect of the redemption on the voting power of the redeemed shareholder, whether the shareholder has the right to participate in current or future earnings, and whether the shareholder has the right to a share of the net assets upon liquidation. See, e.g., Rev. Rul. 81-289, 1981-2 C.B. 82.

■■■

Quicknotes

COMMON STOCK A class of stock representing the corporation's ownership, the holders of which are entitled to dividends only after the holders of preferred stock are paid.

PREFERRED STOCK Shares of stock that are entitled to payment of dividends and other distributions before the holders of common stock.

REDEMPTION The repurchase of a security by the issuing corporation according to the terms specified in the security agreement specifying the procedure for the repurchase.

■■■

Arnes v. United States

Shareholder (P) v. Federal government (D)

981 F.2d 456 (9th Cir. 1992).

NATURE OF CASE: Appeal from summary judgment relieving taxpayer from recognition of gain realized pursuant to a divorce settlement.

FACT SUMMARY: Joann Arnes (P) argued that she should not have to recognize gain on a sale of her stock shares because the transfer was made pursuant to a divorce proceeding.

🏛 RULE OF LAW

A transfer of stock to a corporation made pursuant to a divorce settlement will qualify for nonrecognition of gain if the nontransferring spouse receives a benefit.

FACTS: In 1980, John and Joann (P) Arnes formed a corporation, "Moriah," to operate a McDonald's franchise. Moriah issued 5,000 shares of stock in the names of John and Joann (P). In 1987, the couple agreed to divorce. The McDonald's Corporation required 100% ownership of the equity and profits by the owner/operator and informed John that there should be no joint ownership of the restaurant after the divorce. Joann (P) and John agreed to have their corporation redeem Joann's (P) 50% interest in the outstanding stock for $450,000 by forgiving a debt that she owed to the corporation and paying the remainder to her in monthly installments. The agreement was incorporated into the decree of dissolution of the marriage. Joann (P) thereafter surrendered her 2,500 shares to the corporation. On her federal income tax return for 1988, Joann (P) reported that she sold her stock in Moriah for $450,000 and that her basis was $2,500, resulting in a profit of $447,500. On December 27, 1989, she filed a timely claim for a refund of $53,053 for 1988 on the ground that she was not required to recognize any gain on the transfer of her stock because the transfer was made pursuant to a divorce instrument. The Internal Revenue Service (IRS) (D) did not allow the claim for refund, and Joann (P) sued. The district court found that the redemption of Joann's (P) stock in Moriah was required by the divorce instrument and that John benefited from the transaction because it was part of the marital property settlement and limited future community property claims that Joann (P) might bring against him. The transfer thus qualified for nonrecognition of gain pursuant to the IRC exemption for transfers made to spouses or former spouses incident to a divorce settlement. Joann's (P) motion for summary judgment was granted by the district court. The IRS (D) appealed.

ISSUE: Will the transfer of stock to a corporation made pursuant to a divorce settlement qualify for nonrecognition of gain if the nontransferring spouse receives a benefit?

HOLDING AND DECISION: (Hug, J.) Yes. The transfer of stock to a corporation made pursuant to a divorce settlement qualifies for nonrecognition of gain if the nontransferring spouse receives a benefit. Section 1041 of the Internal Revenue Coe (IRC) provides that: (a) no gain or loss shall be recognized on a transfer of property from an individual to (or in trust for the benefit of) a spouse or a former spouse, but only if the transfer is incident to the divorce; (b) the property shall be treated as acquired by the transferee by gift; and (c) the basis of the transference in the property shall be the adjusted basis of the transferor. The purpose of this provision is to defer the tax consequences between spouses or former spouses. Property received in such a transfer is excluded from the recipient's gross income. The recipient's basis is then equal to the transferor's basis. Later, when the recipient transfers the property to a third party, the gain or loss must be recognized. In addition, the transfer by a spouse to a third party can be treated as a transfer to the other spouse when it is "on behalf of" the other spouse. In this case, John received a benefit because the transfer was part of the marital property agreement that settled any future community property claims that Joann (P) could have asserted against John. The tax result for Joann (P) is the same as if she had conveyed the property directly to John. Affirmed.

▶ ANALYSIS

The IRS also asserted a protective income tax deficiency against John Arnes, who contested the deficiency by filing a petition with the Tax Court. The IRS maintained that although Joann Arnes (P) was the appropriate party to be taxed for the gain at issue, John Arnes should be taxed if the district court's ruling was upheld. Eventually, John Arnes's case was decided in a reviewed opinion of the Tax Court. See *Arnes v. Commissioner*, 102 T.C. 522 (1994). There, the majority held that he had no constructive dividend because he was not absolutely obligated to acquire Joann Arnes's stock. As a result, neither spouse was taxable on the transaction and the Internal Revenue Service (IRS) was effectively whipsawed by the application of different standards to the transferor and nontransferor spouses in the same transaction. In response to this inconsistency in the courts, the IRS amended the § 1041 regulations to provide for greater clarity and certainty in this area by harmonizing the "primary and unconditional obligation" standard for constructive dividends with IRC § 1041's policy.

■■■

Quicknotes

BASIS The value assigned to a taxpayer's costs incurred as the result of acquiring an asset, and used to compute

Continued on next page.

tax amounts toward the transactions in which that asset is involved.

COMMUNITY PROPERTY In community property jurisdictions, refers to all money or property acquired during the term of the marriage in which each spouse has an undivided one-half interest.

GAIN Refers to situation where amount realized exceeds the basis of an asset.

GROSS INCOME The total income earned by an individual or business.

MARITAL PROPERTY Property accumulated by a married couple during the term of their marriage.

Grove v. Commissioner

Shareholder (P) v. Government official (D)

490 F.2d 241 (2d Cir. 1973).

NATURE OF CASE: Appeal from denial of tax deficiency assessment.

FACT SUMMARY: The Commissioner (D) contended the redemption of stock by Grove's (P) corporation, which was held as a charitable gift from Grove (P), constituted a taxable dividend.

🏛 RULE OF LAW
Redemptions of stock that were held by a charitable organization do not constitute a dividend taxable to the donor.

FACTS: Grove (P) donated a life interest in the principal of stock in his corporation to his alma mater, Rensselaer Polytechnic Institute (RPI). He retained the income interest. RPI redeemed the stock and invested the money, paying Grove (P) dividends thereon. Grove (P) declared such as ordinary income. The Commissioner (D) assessed a deficiency, contending the redemption was a taxable dividend. The Tax Court disallowed the deficiency, and the Commissioner (D) appealed.

ISSUE: Does a redemption of stock held by a charitable organization generate a taxable dividend to the donor?

HOLDING AND DECISION: (Kaufman, C.J.) No. The redemption of stock that was the subject of a charitable contribution does not produce a taxable dividend to the donor. The substance of the transaction was that of a charitable donation. Even though the donation was structured to minimize tax liability, it is nonetheless valid. Thus, no dividend was produced. Affirmed.

DISSENT: (Oakes, J.) The substance of the transaction was a distribution to the shareholder. Thus, it was a taxable dividend.

▶ ANALYSIS

The Commissioner (D) challenged this type of transaction several times before accepting defeat. It issued Revenue Ruling 78-197, which indicated a dividend was present only where the corporation could demand redemption from the donee. These transactions are termed "charitable bailouts."

Niedermeyer v. Commissioner

Shareholder (P) v. Government official (D)

U.S. Tax Ct., 62 T.C. 280 (1974); *aff'd per curiam*, 535 F.2d 500 (9th Cir. 1976);

cert. denied, 429 U.S. 1000 (1976).

NATURE OF CASE: Appeal from assessment of tax deficiency.

FACT SUMMARY: Niedermeyer (P) contended its transfer of stock to its family controlled corporation was a nontaxable redemption rather than a dividend.

🏛 RULE OF LAW
A taxpayer's transfer of stock in one corporation controlled by the transfer to another corporation controlled by him for purposes of liquidation will be treated as a dividend.

FACTS: Niedermeyer (P) owned a majority of the voting stock of American Timber and Trading Co. (AT&T). He transferred the stock to Lents Corp. for cash. Lents was owned by Niedermeyer's (P) sons. This transfer was to facilitate Lents' takeover of control of AT&T. Niedermeyer (P) claimed the proceeds as capital gains, yet the Commissioner (D) contended because of the familial relationship, the control of Lents could be attributed to Niedermeyer (P), and thus the disbursement was a dividend. The Commissioner (D) assessed a deficiency, and Niedermeyer (P) sued in Tax Court.

ISSUE: Will the transfer of stock from one corporation to another controlled by the same purpose generate a taxable dividend?

HOLDING AND DECISION: (Sterrett, J.) Yes. A transfer of stock for cash from one corporation to another, both of which are controlled by the transferor, will generate a taxable dividend. Even though Niedermeyer (P) did not personally own a controlling percentage of Lents stock, the control is attributed to him because of his familial relationship with the controlling shareholders. Thus, the transaction generated a taxable dividend and no capital gains treatment is available. The transaction did not fit into any statute describing a redemption, and it was essentially equivalent to a dividend. Decision for the respondent.

▶ ANALYSIS

The court rejected the taxpayer's argument that the attribution rules should not apply. The controlling interest in Lents was owned by one faction of feuding brothers. The taxpayers therefore claimed a "bad blood" exception to the attribution rules. The court found the taxpayer had no fight with either side. Thus, control was attributed to him.

CHAPTER 6

Stock Dividends and Section 306 Stock

Quick Reference Rules of Law

Chamberlin v. Commissioner

Shareholder (P) v. Government official (D)

207 F.2d 462 (6th Cir. 1953); *cert. denied*, 347 U.S. 918 (1954).

NATURE OF CASE: Appeal from tax deficiency assessment.

FACT SUMMARY: The Commissioner (D) contended a preferred stock distribution pursuant to a bailout constituted a taxable dividend.

🏛 RULE OF LAW
The issuance of preferred stock does not generate a taxable dividend merely because the stock is redeemable.

FACTS: Metal Moulding Corporation was caused by its controlling shareholder Chamberlin (P) to issue preferred stock that was immediately redeemable to certain insurance companies which participated in structuring the distribution. The shareholders claimed the preferred stock distribution was nontaxable, yet the Commissioner (D) assessed a deficiency because of the redemption feature. The Tax Court upheld the deficiency, and Chamberlin (P) appealed.

ISSUE: Is the issuance of redeemable preferred stock a taxable dividend?

HOLDING AND DECISION: (Miller, J.) No. The issuance of redeemable preferred stock is not a taxable dividend merely because the stock is redeemable. All formalities of the stock issuance were complied with, and no attack on the validity of such has been made. Merely because the stock was preordained to be redeemed does not make the distribution of the stock, prior to redemption, a taxable event. Thus, the Tax Court erred in assessing the deficiency on this point. Reversed and remanded.

▌ ANALYSIS

The court points out that it is very clear this transaction was structured to avoid taxation. However, as nothing was done in breach of law, the transaction was valid. The preferred stock did not represent capital participation in the corporation. Thus, the distribution was nontaxable upon redemption; however, the proceeds would be taxed. The device used by the taxpayers in this case is known as a preferred stock bailout. Given that both dividends and capital gains currently enjoy the same relatively low tax rate, the advantages from such a bailout have been greatly diminished.

Quicknotes

PREFERRED STOCK Shares of stock that are entitled to payment of dividends and other distributions before the holders of common stock.

TAX DEFICIENCY An unpaid amount of excess tax liability based on a taxpayer's corrected tax amount due less the amount actually paid.

Fireoved v. United States

Shareholder (P) v. Federal government (D)

462 F.2d 1281 (3d Cir. 1972).

NATURE OF CASE: Appeal from denial of tax refund.

FACT SUMMARY: Fireoved (P) contended his receipt of a stock distribution from one corporation he controlled was nontaxable under Internal Revenue Code (IRC) § 306.

🏛 RULE OF LAW
A stock distribution with a general purpose of tax avoidance will not be exempt from taxation under IRC § 306.

FACTS: Fireoved (P) redeemed preferred shares of stock in a corporation, which he treated as a capital gain. The Commissioner (D) contended under § 306 it must be claimed as ordinary income, as the purpose of the issuance and redemption was to avoid federal income tax, taking it outside the exceptions to § 306. Fireoved (P) appealed the denial of a refund.

ISSUE: Will a stock distribution be subject to IRC § 306 if made with the general purpose of avoiding taxation?

HOLDING AND DECISION: (Adams, J.) No. A stock distribution with a general purpose of tax avoidance must be given ordinary income treatment under IRC § 306. The tax avoidance feature takes the transaction out of the business purpose realm and requires the ordinary income treatment. Such was not immunized by Fireoved's (P) previous sale of common stock. Because not all the stock was received at the same time, a pro rata share must be exempt from § 306. Reversed in part; affirmed in part.

▶ ANALYSIS

IRC § 306, giving ordinary income treatment to stock bailout distributions was enacted in response to *Chamberlin v. Commissioner*, 207 F.2d 462 (1953). In that case, the shareholders had preferred stock issued, which was immediately redeemable. The clear import was tax avoidance, and capital gains treatment was given. However, given that there currently is no distinction between the taxation of capital gains and dividends, which equally enjoy a relatively low tax rate, § 306 effectively is not needed, although it is still in the Code.

Quicknotes

COMMON STOCK A class of stock representing the corporation's ownership, the holders of which are entitled to dividends only after the holders of preferred stock are paid.

PREFERRED STOCK Shares of stock that are entitled to payment of dividends and other distributions before the holders of common stock.

PRO RATA In proportion.

CHAPTER 7

Complete Liquidations

Quick Reference Rules of Law

Commissioner v. Court Holding Co.

Federal government (D) v. Corporate taxpayer (P)

324 U.S. 331 (1945).

NATURE OF CASE: Appeal from tax deficiency assessment.

FACT SUMMARY: Court Holding Co. (Court) (P) contended the sale of its sole asset, after its distribution to its shareholders, was not taxable to the corporation.

🏛 RULE OF LAW
A corporation may be taxed for the sale of its asset after distribution to its shareholders if the substance of the transaction indicates it is the actual seller.

FACTS: Court (P) was a corporation with two shareholders and an apartment house as its sole asset. It began to negotiate the sale of the property. However, to avoid adverse tax effects, the property was distributed to the shareholders as a liquidating dividend and then sold. The Commissioner (D) contended that Court (P) was in substance the seller and assessed a deficiency and the Tax Court agreed, but the court of appeals reversed, and the Commissioner (D) appealed.

ISSUE: May a corporation be taxed for the sale of its assets after distribution to its shareholders?

HOLDING AND DECISION: (Black, J.) Yes. A corporation may be taxed for the sale of its assets after its distribution to its shareholders if the substance of the transaction indicates it is the actual seller. The sole motivation behind the dividend was to avoid corporate income tax. All details of the sale were agreed upon prior to the dividend. Thus, the substance of the transaction indicates the corporation was the seller and must bear the tax. Reversed.

▶ ANALYSIS

This case illustrates the maxim of tax law which holds the tax incident falls according to the substance of the transaction. The form will not govern tax liability, and the courts will look through it to determine the actual substance of the transaction. Further, the question presented here was one of fact, and the Tax Court's findings were not clearly erroneous.

■■■■

United States v. Cumberland Public Service Co.

Federal government (D) v. Corporate taxpayer (P)

338 U.S. 451 (1950).

NATURE OF CASE: On writ of certiorari from Court of Claims on tax deficiency assessment.

FACT SUMMARY: Cumberland Public Service Co. (Cumberland) (P), an electricity generator and distributor, dissolved and distributed its physical properties to its shareholders so that they could sell them to a local Tennessee Valley Authority (TVA) cooperative without incurring capital gains tax.

🏛 RULE OF LAW
If the shareholders of a corporation, subsequent to its dissolution, sell physical properties received during a liquidating distribution to a third party, there will be no capital gains tax on the sale.

FACTS: Cumberland (P) generated and distributed electric power in Kentucky using diesel fuel. When a cooperative began to distribute TVA power, Cumberland (P) could not compete. It offered its stock for sale to the cooperative, which was refused but countered with an offer to buy its transmission and distribution equipment. The corporation, to avoid capital gains tax, transferred the equipment in kind to its shareholders in a liquidating distribution and then dissolved. The shareholders then sold the physical properties to the cooperative. The Internal Revenue Service challenged the sale as taxable, alleging that it had been disguised merely to avoid tax liability.

ISSUE: May a corporation avoid capital gains tax on the distribution of its assets in kind to its shareholders if it transfers them as part of a plan of liquidation and dissolution?

HOLDING AND DECISION: (Black, J.) Yes. If the shareholders of a corporation, subsequent to its dissolution, sell physical properties received during a liquidating distribution to a third party, there will be no capital gains tax on the sale. This case differs from the Supreme Court's previous ruling in the *Court Holding Co.* case, 324 U.S. 331 (1945), where the only reason a so-called liquidation occurred was to disguise a corporate sale through use of formalisms to avoid taxation. There, unlike here, an oral agreement of sale by the corporation to a third party was "called off" at the last minute when the capital gains consequences were realized. Although the assets were transferred to the shareholders, the purchase price to the third party remained the same, and the corporation kept a down payment. Here, there was a genuine dissolution and liquidation, and the Court of Claims dispositively found that the sale was made by the stockholders, not the corporation. A subsidiary finding that the major motive was to avoid taxes does not change this holding. Congress itself mandated the disparate results when a corporation, as in Court Holding Co., sells assets and then distributes proceeds

to shareholders and, as here, distributes assets followed by a shareholder sale. Affirmed.

▶ ANALYSIS

The 1954 Code (formerly § 337) attacked this holding by extending the *General Utilities* doctrine to liquidating sales, such that no gain or loss was recognized, regardless of the form of the transaction, when property was sold in liquidation. This rule was reversed entirely in the 1986 Code, which does require recognition of gain or loss as if the property were traded at its fair market value. IRC § 336(a). This results in a double tax cost and taxable events for both shareholder and corporation but does allow a corporation to recognize a loss as well as a gain, subject to limitations under IRC § 336(d), in cases of distributions to related persons and prevention of doubling of precontribution losses.

■=■

Quicknotes

CAPITAL GAIN AND LOSS Gain or loss from the sale or exchange of a capital asset.

LIQUIDATION The reduction to cash of all assets for distribution to creditors.

■=■

George L. Riggs, Inc. v. Commissioner

U.S. Tax Ct., 64 T.C. 474 (1975).

NATURE OF CASE: Petition for nonrecognition of gain under Internal Revenue Code (IRC) § 332.

FACT SUMMARY: By redeeming the common stock of the minority shareholders in its subsidiary, Riggs-Young, Riggs's (P) ownership in the subsidiary grew to exceed 80%, such that it could liquidate Riggs-Young without recognizing gain.

🏛 RULE OF LAW
IRC § 332(a) precludes recognition of gain or loss by a parent corporation when it liquidates a subsidiary it controls.

FACTS: George L. Riggs, Inc. (Riggs) (P) was a holding company that owned 36% of nonvoting preferred and 72% of common stock in its subsidiary Riggs-Young. In late 1967, Riggs's (P) controlling shareholder announced and consummated sale of all operating assets of Riggs-Young. In February 1968, all Riggs-Young preferred stock was redeemed. From late April to late May 1968, Riggs-Young made a tender offer to its minority common shareholders for redemption of their stock, for the stated purpose of eliminating them and providing them cash. In the letter to the shareholders making the tender offer, possible liquidation and dissolution of Riggs-Young was mentioned. Counsel for Riggs (P) and Riggs (P) itself wanted to own more than 80% of Riggs-Young common so it could file a consolidated tax return and possibly seek nonrecognition of gain in liquidation under IRC § 332. By May 9, 1968, enough common stock had been redeemed to increase Riggs's (P) ownership of Riggs-Young to over 80%. On June 20, 1968, the directors adopted a resolution of dissolution of Riggs-Young, and liquidation resulting in over $2 million in distributions was completed by the end of the year. The Internal Revenue Service (D) recognized the gain as taxable and assessed a deficiency.

ISSUE: Under IRC § 332, must a parent seeking nonrecognition of gain on liquidation of a subsidiary own at least 80% of the voting power and common stock of the subsidiary by the time the resolution of dissolution is adopted?

HOLDING AND DECISION: (Drennen, J.) Yes. Under IRC § 332, a parent seeking nonrecognition of gain on liquidation of a subsidiary must own at least 80% of the voting power and common stock of the subsidiary by the time the resolution of dissolution is adopted. IRC § 332(a) precludes recognition of gain or loss by a parent corporation when it liquidates a subsidiary it controls. "Control" is defined as ownership or 80% or more of voting power and common stock in the subsidiary. This "control" must be achieved prior to the date of adoption by the subsidiary shareholders of the formal resolution authorizing distribution of its assets in redemption of all its stock. Here, Riggs (P) was entitled to nonrecognition under § 332(a) because the plan for liquidation of Riggs-Young was not adopted until June 20, 1968,

well after May 9, 1968, the date when Riggs (P) achieved 80% ownership due to the tender offer. Not the possibility of the tender offer itself, the redemption of preferred stock in Riggs-Young (motivated to reduce the number of shareholders and the burden of cumulative dividends), the tender offer letter, or the informal advice of Riggs's (P) attorneys indicated more than a conditional general intent to liquidate—which is not the same as adoption of a plan of liquidation. Further, the "elective" nature of § 332, allowing parent companies to plan and structure buy-outs, precludes the determinative date of "control" from being when the mere intent is established. Ruling for Riggs (P).

▶ ANALYSIS

The 80 percent or greater ownership requirement found in IRC § 332 is used by IRC § 337, which exempts from recognition of gain or loss a liquidating subsidiary that distributes its property to its parent in a complete liquidation to which § 332 applies. This nonrecognition rule, however, does not apply to distributions of property by a liquidating subsidiary to minority shareholders. Such distributions are regarded as distributions in a nonliquidating redemption, so that the subsidiary in such a case would recognize gain, but not loss.

Quicknotes

COMMON STOCK A class of stock representing the corporation's ownership, the holders of which are entitled to dividends only after the holders of preferred stock are paid.

PREFERRED STOCK Shares of stock that are entitled to payment of dividends and other distributions before the holders of common stock.

RESOLUTION A formal opinion of an official group that is adopted by vote.

CHAPTER 8

Taxable Corporate Acquisitions

Quick Reference Rules of Law

Kimbell-Diamond Milling Co. v. Commissioner

Corporate taxpayer (P) v. Government official

U.S. Tax Ct., 14 T.C. 74 (1950).

NATURE OF CASE: Appeal from assessment of tax deficiency.

FACT SUMMARY: Kimbell-Diamond Milling Co. (Kimbell) (P) contended the acquisition of stock and Whaley's subsequent liquidation should be viewed separately and that no taxable transaction occurred.

RULE OF LAW

Where the essential nature of a transaction is the acquisition of property, it will be viewed as a whole, and closely related steps will not be separated.

FACTS: Kimbell (P) sought to acquire Whaley Corporation solely to liquidate it and gain ownership of its assets. It purchased the stock and three days later liquidated the corporation. It contended its basis in the assets should be what Whaley had, as the transaction should be viewed as a stock sale and separate liquidation. The Commissioner (D) contended the entire transaction was a single acquisition of property, and thus the basis equaled the price paid.

ISSUE: If the essential nature of a transaction is the acquisition of property, may it be viewed separately from its stock acquisition predecessor?

HOLDING AND DECISION: (Black, J.) No. Where the essential nature of a transaction is the acquisition of property, it will be viewed as whole, and closely related steps will not be separated. In this case, Kimbell's (P) admitted purpose in acquiring Whaley was to obtain its assets. Thus, the preliminary stock transfer cannot be viewed separately, and the basis cannot be transferred. Thus, the basis to Kimbell (P) must be based on its contribution to the acquisition.

ANALYSIS

Kimbell's (P) argument, if it had been successful, would have allowed it to obtain an inflated transferred basis in the property. The purchase of stock was not relied upon, however, and the substance of the transaction controlled. The "intent" rule of this decision was replaced with a more objective standard, codified in § 334 of the 1954 Code, but even this section had problems, which Congress attempted to rectify with the enactment of § 338, which permits an acquiring corporation to elect to treat certain stock purchases as asset purchases, sot that liquidation is not necessary for the acquiror to get a cost basis in the acquired assets.

Quicknotes

ASSET An item of real or personal property that is owned and has tangible value.

LIQUIDATION The reduction to cash of all assets for distribution to creditors

TAX DEFICIENCY An unpaid amount of excess tax liability based on a taxpayer's corrected tax amount due less the amount actually paid.

Acquisitive Reorganizations

Quick Reference Rules of Law

Southwest Natural Gas Co. v. Commissioner

Corporate taxpayer (P) v. Government official (D)

189 F.2d 332 (5th Cir. 1951).

NATURE OF CASE: Appeal of determination of non-reorganization in an acquisition.

FACT SUMMARY: Peoples Gas & Fuel Corporation "merged" with Southwest Natural Gas Co. (P) in a transaction wherein 99% of the consideration paid to Peoples' stockholders was nonequity.

🏛 RULE OF LAW
A merger proper by state law standards does not necessarily imply a reorganization for income tax purposes.

FACTS: Peoples Gas & Fuel Corporation (Peoples) merged with Southwest Natural Gas Co. (Southwest) (P). The transaction met state statutory requirements to be classified as a merger. A significant share of Peoples' shareholders was compensated by cash and equity disbursements. The equity given by Southwest (P) amounted to less than 1% of all consideration. The Internal Revenue Service (IRS) (D) denied favorable tax treatment of the transaction, classifying it as a sale. Southwest (P) challenged this in Tax Court. The court held the transaction a sale for tax purposes. Southwest (P) appealed.

ISSUE: Does a merger proper by state law standards necessarily imply a reorganization for income tax purposes?

HOLDING AND DECISION: (Russell, J.) No. A merger proper by state law standards does not necessarily imply a reorganization for income tax purposes. The rationale behind the statutory favorable treatment accorded to mergers is that tax should not be levied on a transaction involving a continuity of interest where any realization is basically on paper. Thus, if a transaction involves a significant change of interest, this favorable tax treatment is inappropriate, regardless of how a jurisdiction labels the transaction. Here, former equity holders of Peoples received almost exclusively cash or debt instruments rather than equity, so there was no continuity of ownership. Affirmed.

▶ ANALYSIS

The transaction here involved what is called a "Type A" reorganization. This label applies to mergers and consolidations. The courts have developed the "continuity of interest" test regarding whether a transaction is truly deserving of favorable tax treatment.

■■■■

Quicknotes

MERGER The acquisition of one company by another, after which the acquired company ceases to exist as an independent entity.

■■■■

J.E. Seagram Corp. v. Commissioner

Corporate taxpayer (P) v. Government official (D)

U.S. Tax Ct., 104 T.C. 75 (1995).

NATURE OF CASE: Cross-motion for summary judgment in action challenging claimed loss on an exchange of corporate stocks.

FACT SUMMARY: J.E. Seagram Corp. (Seagram) (P) challenged the Internal Revenue Service's (IRS) (D) disallowance of a loss Seagram (P) claimed on the exchange of stock acquired in Conoco, Inc. after Seagram (P) and DuPont became involved in a multistep takeover contest for Conoco.

🏛 RULE OF LAW
When a party is contractually obligated to complete a second-step merger once it has completed a first-step tender offer, these integrated transactions constitute a plan of reorganization resulting in no recognition of loss on an accompanying exchange of stock.

FACTS: In 1981, Seagram (P), after an unsuccessful attempt to negotiate a friendly takeover of Conoco, commenced a cash tender offer for Conoco stock. Two weeks later, DuPont and Conoco entered into an agreement for a two-step acquisition under which a DuPont subsidiary commenced a competing tender offer to acquire all of Conoco's stock in exchange for a combination of cash and stock, to be followed by a merger of Conoco into a DuPont subsidiary. The agreement was subject to several conditions, including the requirement that at least 51% of Conoco's stock be tendered. After various other tender offers expired, Seagram (P) acquired 32% of Conoco's stock for cash, but DuPont acquired more than 50% through its tender offer. Seagram (P) tendered its 32% Conoco stake to DuPont in exchange for DuPont stock, realizing an economic loss of more than $500 million, which Seagram (P) claimed. The IRS (D) disallowed the loss on the ground that the integrated transaction constituted a tax-free acquisitive reorgani-zation. Seagram (P) filed an action challenging the IRS's (D) disallowance of the loss, and both Seagram (P) and the IRS (D) filed motions for summary judgment.

ISSUE: When a party is contractually obligated to complete a second-step merger once it has completed a first-step tender offer, do these integrated transactions constitute a plan of reorganization for tax purposes?

HOLDING AND DECISION: (Nims, J.) Yes. When a party is contractually obligated to complete a second-step merger once it has completed a first-step tender offer, these integrated transactions constitute a plan of reorganization for tax purposes. Under § 368(a)(1)(A) of the Internal Revenue Code, the term "reorganization" means (1) a statutory merger or consolidation, and (2) the acquisition by one corporation in exchange for stock of a corporation which is in control of the acquiring corporation, of substantially all of the properties of another corporation shall not disqualify a transaction under paragraph (1)(A) if no stock of the acquiring corporation is used in the transaction and such transaction would have qualified under paragraph (1)(A) had the merger been into the controlling corporation. Here, the merger of Conoco into the DuPont subsidiary complied with requirements of Delaware law, thus meeting this description of "reorganization." Seagram (P), however, claims that DuPont's tender offer and the subsequent merger squeezing out the remaining Conoco shareholders were separate and independent transactions. Therefore, the exchange of Conoco stock for DuPont stock pursuant to DuPont's tender offer rather than pursuant to the merger could not have been in pursuance of a plan of reorganization. However, the overall transaction did include the merger. Therefore, Seagram's (P) conclusion that there was no reorganization is incorrect. Furthermore, the concept of a "plan of reorganization" is one of substantial elasticity. Here, also, the requirement that in a reorganization under § 368(a)(1)(A) there must be "continuity of interest" is satisfied. The reorganization provisions are based on the premise that the shareholders of an acquired corporation have not terminated their economic investment but have merely altered its form. Thus, the "continuity of interest" doctrine limits the favorable nonrecognition treatment enjoyed by reorganizations to those situations in which (1) the nature of the consideration received by the acquired corporation or its shareholders confers a proprietary stake in the ongoing enterprise, and (2) the proprietary interest received is definite and material and represents a substantial part of the value of the property transferred. In the "integrated" transaction before us, Seagram (P), not DuPont, stepped into the shoes of 32% of the Conoco shareholders when Seagram (P) acquired their stock for cash via the competing tender offer, held the 32% transitorily and immediately tendered it in exchange for DuPont stock. For present purposes, there is no material distinction between Seagram's (P) tender of their Conoco stock and a direct tender by the "old" Conoco shareholders themselves. Thus the requirement of continuity of interest has been met. Seagram's (P) conduct is inconsistent with the recognized loss claimed on its tax return. Seagram's (P) motion for summary judgment is denied, and the IRS's (D) motion for summary judgment is granted.

▶ ANALYSIS

Seagram (P) also argued that the "continuity of interest" doctrine under § 368(a)(1)(A) required that the identity of an acquired corporation's shareholders be tracked to ensure a sufficient number of "historic" shareholders to satisfy a minimal percentage receiving the acquiring corporation's stock. The IRS and the Tax Court both pointed out that this

Continued on next page.

interpretation was unrealistic and that the U.S. Supreme Court had rejected such an interpretation in *Helvering v. Alabama Asphaltic Limestone Co.*, 315 U.S. 179 (1942). In *Alabama Asphaltic,* unsecured noteholders of an insolvent corporation commenced a bankruptcy proceeding against a corporation. The noteholders bought the corporate assets from the trustee and transferred them to a newly formed corporation in exchange for its stock. The Court stated that when the equity owners are excluded and the old creditors become the stockholders of the new corporation, it conforms to realities to date their equity ownership from the time when they invoked the processes of the law to enforce their rights of full priority. At that time, they "stepped into the shoes" of the old stockholders, and the sale did nothing but recognize officially what had before been true in fact.

■===■

Quicknotes

MERGER The acquisition of one company by another, after which the acquired company ceases to exist as an independent entity.

TENDER OFFER An offer made by one corporation to the shareholders of a target corporation to purchase their shares subject to number, time, and price specifications.

■===■

Bentsen v. Phinney

Shareholder (P) v. Government official (D)

199 F. Supp. 363 (S.D. Tex. 1961).

NATURE OF CASE: Action for tax refund.

FACT SUMMARY: Bentsen (P) and others exchanged stock in a land development company for stock in an insurance company and sought a refund of taxes assessed on the transactions.

RULE OF LAW
To qualify as a reorganization under relevant statutes, the new corporation does not have to engage in an identical or similar business as that of the old.

FACTS: Bentsen (P) and others were shareholders in various corporations engaged in land development. The corporations were dissolved and the assets and liabilities transferred to a new corporation formed to sell life insurance. Because the new corporation did not engage in the same sort of business as did the old corporations, the Internal Revenue Service (IRS) (D) held the transaction taxable. Bentsen (P) and the others brought an action in district court to recover the taxes paid.

ISSUE: To qualify as a reorganization under relevant statutes, does the new corporation have to engage in an identical or similar business as that of the old?

HOLDING AND DECISION: (Garza, J.) No. To qualify as a reorganization under relevant statutes, the new corporation does not have to engage in an identical or similar business as that of the old. For a reorganization to be nontaxable there must be a continuity of business enterprise. The IRS (D) contends that this means that the same type of business must be carried on. However, there is no statutory authority for this, and what little case law exists suggests that courts have refused to adopt this position, although no court has directly passed on this issue. This court is of the opinion that the meaning urged by the IRS (D) is too restrictive. Judgment for Bentsen (P) et al.

ANALYSIS

The issue in this case arose under Internal Revenue Code § 368(a)(1). The IRS (D) has ruled that in a § 368(a)(1) reorganization, the continuity of business enterprise requirement does not apply to the business or business assets of the transferee corporation prior to the reorganization.

■=■

Chapman v. Commissioner

Shareholder (P) v. Government official (D)

618 F.2d 856 (1st Cir. 1980).

NATURE OF CASE: Appeal of Tax Court finding of nontaxable reorganization.

FACT SUMMARY: ITT, Inc. first purchased 8% of Hartford Fire Insurance's stock, then acquired over 80% more in a stock-for-stock acquisition.

🏛 RULE OF LAW

A transaction where one corporation purchases stock in another and also acquires over 80% in a stock-for-stock exchange is not a nontaxable reorganization.

FACTS: ITT, Inc. developed an interest in purchasing Hartford Fire Insurance, Inc. Hartford's management at first resisted the overture. Nonetheless, in a series of cash purchases, ITT purchased 8% of Hartford stock on the open market. An agreement was reached whereby Hartford shareholders would exchange their stock for ITT stock. This was done, and Hartford became an ITT subsidiary. The Internal Revenue Service (IRS) (D) held this to be a taxable transaction and further held that capital gains tax must be imposed. Various former Hartford shareholders (P) challenged this in the Tax Court. The court held that the transaction was a nontaxable reorganization. The IRS (D) appealed.

ISSUE: Is a transaction where one corporation purchases stock in another and also acquires over 80% in a stock-for-stock exchange a nontaxable reorganization?

HOLDING AND DECISION: (Campbell, J.) No. A transaction where one corporation purchases stock in another and also acquires over 80% in a stock-for-stock exchange is not a nontaxable reorganization. Section 368(a)(B) exempts from taxation a transaction wherein one corporation acquires, solely in exchange for voting stock, the stock of another corporation, and the acquiring corporation has control of the acquired corporation following the transaction. "Control" is defined as at least 80% of the voting shares and 80% of all outstanding shares. The plain meaning of this is that the acquiring corporation must give nothing other than voting stock to shareholders of the acquired corporation. Any other form of consideration will take the transaction out of § 368(a)(1)(B). Legislative history in this area is quite complex and sometimes confusing, as several different, competing policies were juggled. For this reason, a court should not lightly read a meaning into a statute not readily found there. Also, the weight of authority, both in IRS (D) pronouncements and case law, favors this interpretation. In an area such as tax law, where predictability is vital, a departure from precedent should not be made unless a clear congressional

purpose is found, which is not the case here. Vacated and remanded.

▶ ANALYSIS

The type of reorganization involved in this case is known as a Type B reorganization, which is on involving acquisitions of stock solely for voting stock. The general rule, as made clear by the court of appeals in the case, is that there can be no boot in a Type B reorganization. Although the IRS (D) attempted to also disqualify from B reorganizations those in which contingent rights to acquire additional stock were involved, the courts did not support this position, and the IRS has conceded that such consideration will not disqualify B reorganization. As the court in this case indicated, the legislative history in this area is quite complex. The reorganization concept was introduced into tax law in 1924. It was amended in 1939 and 1954. Each amendment followed a lengthy hearing process wherein the merits of tax-free reorganizations were heavily debated. The code sections ultimately evidenced heavy compromise.

■■■

Quicknotes

SUBSIDIARY A company, a majority of whose shares are owned by another corporation and which is subject to that corporation's control.

■■■

Bercy Industries, Inc. v. Commissioner

Corporate taxpayer (P) v. Government official (D)

640 F.2d 1058 (9th Cir. 1981).

NATURE OF CASE: Appeal of a challenge to an Internal Revenue Service (IRS) (D) deficiency assessment.

FACT SUMMARY: The IRS (D) denied a loss carryback on a corporation formed after a triangular merger.

🏛 RULE OF LAW
A subsidiary corporation in a triangular merger may carry back postmerger losses to offset premerger income of the transferor corporation, where the subsidiary was a mere shell before the merger.

FACTS: Beverly Enterprises had a shell subsidiary, Beverly Manor. By way of a triangular merger, (old) Bercy Industries was merged into Beverly Manor, which renamed itself (new) Bercy Industries (P). The shareholders of old Bercy exchanged their stock for shares of Beverly Enterprises. New Bercy (P) continued the same enterprise as did old Bercy. New Bercy (P) suffered losses. New Bercy (P) attempted to carry back its losses to profits of old Bercy. The IRS (D) disallowed the carryback, and the Tax Court agreed with the IRS (D). Bercy (P) appealed.

ISSUE: May a subsidiary corporation in a triangular merger carry back postmerger losses to offset premerger income of the transferor corporation, where the subsidiary was a mere shell before the merger?

HOLDING AND DECISION: (Trask, J.) Yes. A subsidiary corporation in a triangular merger may carry back postmerger losses to offset premerger income of the transferor corporation, where the subsidiary was a mere shell before the merger. Recognizing the long-term nature of business operations, Congress enacted § 172 of the Tax Code, which permits corporations to carry back or forward annual losses. Concerned that corporations would abuse this by absorbing corporations with losses, Congress also enacted § 381, which places certain restrictions on loss carrybacks following mergers. The statute does not precisely address the situation here. However, legislative history demonstrates that where there is no problem with complex allocation of losses, carrybacks should be permitted. Here, Old Bercy and New Bercy (P) both engaged in the same sort of business, and therefore there is no problem with loss allocation. For this reason, there is no policy rationale for refusing the loss carryback. Reversed.

▶ ANALYSIS

As stated in the opinion, § 381 was enacted to prevent abusive tax avoidance schemes involving mergers of losing corporations into profitable ones. Section 381 prevents, for instance, premerger profits from being weighed against the losses of the newly merged corporation. Other possible avoidance techniques are guarded against in § 381.

■■■

Quicknotes

MERGER The acquisition of one company by another, after which the acquired company ceases to exist as an independent entity.

SUBSIDIARY A company, a majority of whose shares are owned by another corporation and which is subject to that corporation's control.

■■■

CHAPTER 10

Corporate Divisions

Quick Reference Rules of Law

Gregory v. Helvering

Shareholder (P) v. Government official (D)

293 U.S. 465 (1935).

NATURE OF CASE: Appeal of tax deficiency assessment.

FACT SUMMARY: Gregory (P) created a corporation for the sole purpose of effecting a tax-deferred reorganization.

🏛 RULE OF LAW
A transaction meeting the statutory prerequisites for a reorganization will not be so recognized if it was purely a tax avoidance device with no business purpose.

FACTS: Gregory (P) was sole shareholder of United Mortgage Company. Gregory (P) created Averill Corporation, of which she was also sole shareholder. United transferred to Averill 1,000 shares of stock it held in Monitor Corporation. Averill was then liquidated, with its assets, the Monitor stock, transferred to Gregory (P). Gregory (P), on her tax return, characterized this as a reorganization, which was nontaxable. The Internal Revenue Service (IRS) (D) disagreed and assessed a deficiency. The Board of Tax Appeals held it a legitimate reorganization. The court of appeals reversed. The Supreme Court accepted review.

ISSUE: Will a transaction meeting the statutory prerequisites for a reorganization be so recognized if it was purely a tax avoidance device with no business purpose?

HOLDING AND DECISION: (Sutherland, J.) No. A transaction meeting the statutory prerequisites for a reorganization will not be so recognized if it was purely a tax avoidance device with no business purpose. It is the right of every taxpayer to frame his transactions in such a manner as to pay the least tax. However, if the transaction is nothing more than an artifice designed to avoid taxes, having no business purpose other than that, courts will look beyond mere form. Here, the transaction met the statutory prerequisites for a reorganization under Tax Code § 112(g). However, the transaction was nothing more than a taxable conveyance of stock through the contrivance of a corporation that was never intended to serve any other purpose. This was not what Congress intended to receive favorable tax treatment, and it will not be given in this instance. Affirmed.

▌ ANALYSIS

The instant case was an important one in the history of tax law as it was one of the earliest cases to articulate the substance over form and step doctrines. The early code sections regarding reorganizations and spin-offs were fraught with possibilities for abusive avoidance techniques. In this case, the Supreme Court gave its approval to courts looking beyond the form of a transaction and into the substance.

Quicknotes

DEFICIENCY Refers to amount of tax taxpayer owes, or is claimed to owe, the IRS.

Lockwood's Estate v. Commissioner

Deceased shareholder's estate (P) v. Government official (D)

350 F.2d 712 (8th Cir. 1965).

NATURE OF CASE: Appeal from Tax Court ruling disallowing tax-free status under § 355(b)(2)(B).

FACT SUMMARY: Lockwood (P) established a branch office of his potato machinery business in Maine and distributed the new corporation's stock in reliance on the tax-free provision of § 355(b)(2)(B). However, the Tax Court held that this distribution fell outside of the provision.

🏛 RULE OF LAW
A spinoff corporation may be eligible for tax-free status under § 355(b)(2)(B) if its distributing corporation had been actively conducting the type of business now performed by the spinoff corporation for five years prior to the distribution.

FACTS: Lockwood (P), deceased, and his wife Margaret were the sole stockholders of the Lockwood Grader Corporation of Nebraska, incorporated in 1946, a business engaged in the manufacturing and selling of wash lines, potato machinery, and other parts and supplies to potato shippers. Lockwood (P) gradually opened branches in several states, and in the early 1950s altered the nature of the business by selling to individual farmers as well as potato suppliers. In 1952, under a reorganization plan, the various branches were separately incorporated to promote greater efficiency and to make use of the tax-free provisions of what would become § 355(b)(2)(B). In November 1954 a branch office was established in Maine, and in March 1956 the branch was incorporated under the laws of Maine. The shares were distributed between the Lockwoods (P), giving rise to the controversy contained herein. The Tax Court held that the distribution was outside of § 355(b)(2)(B) because the Maine business was not actively and continuously conducted until August 1953, thereby not meeting the five-year active business requirement of the provision. Lockwood's (P) estate appealed.

ISSUE: May a spinoff corporation be eligible for tax-free status under § 355(b)(2)(B) if its distributing corporation had been actively conducting the type of business now performed by the spinoff corporation for five years prior to the distribution?

HOLDING AND DECISION: (Vogel, J.) Yes. A spinoff corporation may be eligible for tax-free status under § 355(b)(2)(B) if its distributing corporation had been actively conducting the type of business now performed by the spinoff corporation for five years prior to the distribution. The five years of prior activity that the Tax Court should have taken into account involve the prior overall activity of Lockwood's (P) corporations, not merely the Maine spinoff. Contrary to the assertions of the Tax Court, Congress has never intimated that a geographical test be used so that only Lockwood's (P) activities in the Northeast region would be relevant. The Tax Court erred in determining that the transfer was not tax-free. Reversed.

▶ ANALYSIS

The history of the tax-free spinoff prior to § 355(b)(2)(B) is a varied one. While prior to 1924, and between 1934 and 1950, distributions to stockholders pursuant to a spinoff were taxed, for a brief time between 1924 and 1934 revenue acts permitted the spinoffs to be tax-free. They were abolished after this period, however, because of the use of the exemption as a way to avoid paying taxes on profits. When § 355 of the Code was enacted in 1954, safeguards such as the five-year active business requirement were added to prevent such abuses from recurring. The Internal Revenue Service has held that the creation by a corporation engaged in a certain retail business of a website that sells the same product as the retail store constitutes an expansion of the retail business rather than the acquisition of a new or different business under § 355. See Rev. Rul. 2003-38.

CHAPTER 11

Nonacquisitive, Nondivisive Reorganizations

Quick Reference Rules of Law

Bazley v. Commissioner

Shareholder (P) v. Government official (D)

331 U.S. 737 (1947).

NATURE OF CASE: Appeal from decision finding distribution of debentures pursuant to recapitalization taxable as earned income.

FACT SUMMARY: Bazley (P) appealed from a court of appeals decision that the reorganization of the family business had no legitimate business purpose and was, therefore, not a reorganization under the statute, and the distribution of debentures to Bazley (P) pursuant to this reorganization was a disguised dividend, taxable as earned income.

🏛 RULE OF LAW
When the reorganization of a business serves no legitimate business purpose, the distribution of debentures pursuant to the business's recapitalization is a taxable distribution.

FACTS: Bazley (P) and his wife owned all but one of the company's outstanding shares that had a par value of $100. Pursuant to the plan of reorganization, these old shares were turned in, and Bazley (P) received new shares and debenture bonds with a face value of $319,200. The earned surplus at the time of the transaction was $855,783.82. The Commissioner (D) charged to Bazley (P) as income the full value of the debentures and issued an income tax deficiency against Bazley (P). The tax court affirmed, finding that the reorganization had no legitimate business purpose and was, therefore, not a reorganization under the statute and also holding that the distribution of debentures was a disguised dividend that was taxable. The court of appeals affirmed, and Bazley (P), contending that the issuance of debentures should be exempt from taxation as part of a plan of reorganization, appealed.

ISSUE: When the reorganization of a business serves no legitimate business purpose, is the distribution of debentures pursuant to the business's recapitalization a taxable distribution?

HOLDING AND DECISION: (Frankfurter, J.) Yes. When the reorganization of a business serves no legitimate business purpose, the distribution of debentures pursuant to the business's recapitalization is a taxable distribution. The term "recapitalization" must be construed with reference to the purposes behind the provision affording preferential tax treatment to exchanges of stock or securities made pursuant to a plan of reorganization. The recapitalization in the present case appears to be in form only; there did not seem to be any significant change in the rights and relations of the interested parties to each other or to the company. The purpose of the reorganization appears to have been to accomplish distribution of earnings. Had the debentures been issued to Bazley (P) without any recapitalization, there would have clearly been a taxable distribution. Nothing was accomplished by the reorganization that could not have been accomplished by an outright debenture dividend. In the present case, the reorganization is not a reorganization under the statute and should be considered a taxable distribution. Affirmed.

▶ ANALYSIS

The Court in the present case seems to adopt a sort of disguised dividend theory. It was important to the decision that the amount of earned surplus at the time of the issuance of the debentures exceeded the face value of the debentures. In the present case, the shareholders received new bonds on a pro rata basis. There is some indication that an exchange of stock for bonds on a non-pro rata basis might be successful. See *Seide v. C.I.R.*, 18 T.C. 502 (1952).

◼◼◼

Quicknotes

DEBENTURES Long-term unsecured debt securities issued by a corporation.

RECAPITALIZATION The restructuring of the capital of a corporation.

◼◼◼

Smothers v. United States

Shareholder (P) v. Federal government (D)

642 F.2d 894 (5th Cir. 1981).

NATURE OF CASE: Appeal of challenge to deficiency assessment.

FACT SUMMARY: The Smotherses (P) transferred 15% of the assets of a wholly owned corporation to another wholly owned corporation and then liquidated it.

RULE OF LAW
A transaction may qualify as a "D" reorganization even if only a small percentage of tangible assets are transferred.

FACTS: The Smotherses (P) operated TIL, a corporation in the industrial laundry business. They also owned and operated IUS, an industrial uniform business. At one point they created a transaction whereby IUS's tangible assets were transferred to TIL, and IUS was liquidated. TIL absorbed both IUS's business and its employees. The Smotherses (P) treated this as a liquidation, taxed at capital gains rates. The Internal Revenue Service (IRS) (D) considered it a reorganization, with the cash assets transferred to the Smotherses (P) being treated as a taxable dividend. The tangible assets transferred to TIL had been about 15% of IUS's assets. The tax court held in favor of the IRS (D), and the Smotherses (P) appealed.

ISSUE: May a transaction qualify as a "D" reorganization even if only a small percentage of tangible assets are transferred?

HOLDING AND DECISION: (Wisdom, J.) Yes. A transaction may qualify as a "D" reorganization even if only a small percentage of tangible assets are transferred. Because dividends are taxed at ordinary rates and liquidations at capital gains rates, taxpayers often try to mask a dividend as a liquidation. Reincorporation, wherein a corporation is dissolved, its liquid assets taken and then resurrected, is one such technique. The transaction here was one such effort. However, the transaction qualifies, under § 368(a)(1)(D), as a reorganization. Section 368(a)(1)(D) requires that "substantially all" the assets of the transferor corporation be transferred. The Smotherses (P) argue that 15% was not "substantially all" of IUS's assets. However, "substantially all" should be read to mean assets sufficient for the transferee to carry on the transferor's business. This is the case here; IUS's business was primarily a service that did not require a good deal of equipment, and TIL was able to carry on its enterprise with what it received. For this reason, the transaction qualifies as a "D" reorganization. Affirmed.

DISSENT: (Garza, J.) The majority has changed the statutory requisite from "substantially all assets" to "necessary operating assets." This is the role of Congress, not the courts.

ANALYSIS

The IRS (D) has issued temporary regulations that provide that an acquisitive transaction can be a Type D reorganization even if no stock of the transferee corporation is issued and distributed in the transaction when the same person or persons own, directly and indirectly, all the stock of the transferor and transferee corporations in identical proportions. See Reg. § 1.368-2T(l)(2)(i).

Quicknotes

DEFICIENCY Refers to amount of tax taxpayer owes, or is claimed to owe, the IRS.

LIQUIDATION The reduction to cash of all assets for distribution to creditors.

CHAPTER 12

Limitations on Carryovers of Corporate Attributes

Quick Reference Rules of Law

Garber Industries Holding Co., Inc. v. Commissioner

Corporate taxpayer (P) v. Government official (D)

U.S. Tax Ct., 124 T.C. 1 (2005).

NATURE OF CASE: Petition challenging federal tax deficiency.

FACT SUMMARY: Garber Industries Holding Co., Inc. (Garber) (P) contended that when Kenneth Garber sold all of his shares in Garber (P) to his brother Charles Garber, thereby raising Charles's interest in the company from 19% to 84%, that transaction did not constitute an ownership change for purposes of Internal Revenue Code (IRC) § 382 and therefore did not trigger that section's limitation on net operating loss (NOL) carryovers.

RULE OF LAW

A stock sale between siblings that increases one sibling's percentage ownership of a corporate taxpayer by more than 50 percentage points results in an ownership change for purposes of IRC § 382, triggering that section's limitation on net operating loss carryovers, where none of the siblings' parents or grandparents have been shareholders of the loss corporation.

FACTS: In 1998, Kenneth Garber sold all his shares in Garber Industries Holding Co., Inc. (Garber) (P) to his brother Charles Garber, thereby raising Charles's interest in the company from 19% to 84%. None of the siblings' parents or grandparents had been Garber (P) shareholders, nor were any of these relatives alive in the three years before 1998. On its 1998 consolidated federal income tax return, Garber (P) claimed a $808,935 net operating loss (NOL) deduction for regular tax purposes and $728,041 for alternative minimum tax (AMT) purposes. The Internal Revenue Service (IRS) (D) adjusted the amount of these NOL deductions, for both regular tax and AMT purposes, to $121,258 pursuant to IRC § 382(b). Garber (P) challenged the federal tax deficiency that resulted from the NOL deduction adjustment in the U.S. Tax Court, which granted review.

ISSUE: Does a stock sale between siblings that increases one sibling's percentage ownership of a corporate taxpayer by more than 50 percentage points result in an ownership change for purposes of IRC § 382, triggering that section's limitation on net operating loss carryovers, where none of the siblings' parents or grandparents have been shareholders of the loss corporation?

HOLDING AND DECISION: (Halpern, J.) Yes. A stock sale between siblings that increases one sibling's percentage ownership of a corporate taxpayer by more than 50 percentage points results in an ownership change for purposes of IRC § 382, triggering that section's limitation on net operating loss carryovers, where none of the

siblings' parents or grandparents have been shareholders of the loss corporation. IRC § 382(a) provides that certain ownership changes in a corporation limit the amount of net operating losses (NOLs) the corporation (called a "loss corporation") may deduct. An ownership change for purposes of IRC § 382 generally occurs where, on a required measurement date (a testing date), the aggregate percentage ownership interest of one or more 5% shareholders of the loss corporation is more than 50 percentage points greater than the lowest percentage ownership interest of such shareholder(s) during the 3-year period immediately preceding such testing date (the testing period). Under IRC § 382(l)(3)(A)(i), a special family attribution rule is created whereby an individual and all members of his family described in IRC § 318(a)(1) (spouse, children, grandchildren, and parents) are treated as one individual. Tax regulations further provide that if an individual may be treated as a member of more than one family, such individual will be treated as a member of the family with the smallest increase in percentage ownership (to the exclusion of all other families). Accordingly, Garber (P) argues that even though Kenneth and Charles are not family members described in IRC § 318(a)(1), Charles and Kenneth are nonetheless members of the same family when such determination is made by reference to their parents and grandparents, so that transactions between them should be disregarded for purposes of IRC § 382. The IRS (D) counters that the family aggregation rule applies solely with reference to living individuals, and since none of the parents and grandparents were alive at the commencement of the 3-year testing period immediately preceding the 1998 transaction, from that point forward there was no individual under the apposite statutes whose family members included both Charles and Kenneth. Therefore, the IRS (D) concludes that the brothers are not treated as a single individual, and that there was an ownership change for purposes of limiting NOL deductions. To determine the outcome of this dispute, the initial inquiry is whether the plain language of IRC § 382(l)(3)(A)(i) supports (or precludes) either party's position. That section, in pertinent part, indicates that "an individual and all members of his family . . . shall be treated as one individual. . . ." The IRS (D) argues that the word "individual" (in the first part of the section) does not include a deceased parent. However, this is too a narrow a focus, as words must be interpreted in context. Instead, the question is whether the language of this section as a whole definitively establishes, one way or the other, that the identification of an individual, whether living or deceased, whose family members are aggregated under the section must be made, as the IRS (D) maintains, or does not need to be made, as

Continued on next page.

Garber (P) maintains, coincident with the determination of stock ownership on a testing date or at any point during a testing period. The section is ambiguous on this point, and can accommodate both parties' positions. Therefore, the legislative history and other evidence may be looked to for guidance. The section was amended as part of the Tax Reform Act of 1986. Prior to amendment, the section excluded intrafamily sales from the NOL deduction limitations by means of stock attribution rather than shareholder aggregation rules. Also, ownership changes were ascertained by reference to the holdings of the 10 largest shareholders at the end of the corporation's taxable year. Thus, although family members were potentially subject to aggregation for purposes of determining the 10 largest shareholders at year end, that rule applied only if loss corporation stock owned by one was attributed to the other under the family attribution rules of IRC § 318. This meant that the aggregation rule necessarily applied as of yearend. Therefore, no inference can be drawn from the previous version of the section as to whether the identification of the individuals whose family members are aggregated under IRC § 382(l)(3)(A)(i) occurs as of the date on which stock ownership is measured. The next step is to ascertain the consequences of each party's position and assess whether Congress likely intended such consequences. Under Garber's (P) position, an individual would be aggregated with—and could sell loss corporation stock with no NOL deduction limitations to—not only his spouse, children, grandchildren, and parents, but also his siblings, nephews, nieces, grandparents, in-laws, great-grandchildren, aunts, uncles, first cousins, and great-grandparents. It is unlikely Congress intended to expand the exemption for intrafamily sales of stock so broadly. As for the IRS's (D) position, not only does it have the potential for being just as expansive as Garber's (P) position, but it would also require that the ability of siblings to sell loss corporation shares among themselves without any NOL deduction limitations depends entirely on whether the parents are alive or deceased. There is no rational basis for such a distinction. Thus, both parties' positions miss the mark. Instead, what Congress most likely intended is that the aggregation rule apply solely from the perspective of individuals who are shareholders—as determined under the attribution rules of IRC § 382(l)(3)(A)—of the loss corporation. This interpretation is supported by the changes effected by the amendment of IRC § 382, which put in place the concept of the "owner shift," defined broadly to include any change in the respective ownership of the stock of a corporation. Under this concept, the requisite increase in stock ownership within the resulting testing period does not have to be attributable to a purchase, redemption, or any transaction in which shares actually change hands. Under the prior version of the section, this owner shift concept could have thus caused artificial ownership increases through the application of the family attribution rules of IRC § 318(a), as where marriage of a loss corporation's only shareholder to a nonshareholder (to whom the shareholder's shares would be completely attributed) would result in a change of ownership. In attempting to address such a situation, a proposed

legislative "fix" was to provide that the family status at the close of the testing period was the same as at the beginning of the testing period. This version was not included in the final amended statute, so that the artificial ownership increases could still occur under the interpretations propounded by each party. However, the omission of this proposed provision does not permit artificial ownership increases if the family aggregation rule applies solely from the perspective of shareholders of the loss corporation. Such an interpretation also does not conflict with the plain language of IRC § 382(l)(3)(A)(i) since, in context of that statute, it is not an interpretive stretch that the set of individuals contemplated by Congress (i.e., individuals who own shares of the loss corporation) is smaller than the universe of all possible individuals (i.e., all living beings). This interpretation is further supported by the legislative history, since the final statute included "grandparents" rather than "grandchildren" as members of the family with whom the "individual" could be aggregated. Such a substitution makes sense when viewed from the perspective of shareholders of the loss corporation. This substitution suggests that Congress intended individuals to be aggregated with the same family members to whom their shares would otherwise be attributed. Such an interpretation also does not conflict with IRS (D) regulations. Moreover, such an interpretation does not vitiate the tiebreaker rule of those regulations, which serves to precluded purely "vicarious" ownership increases that could otherwise occur under any of the interpretations of the statute presented here. Applying IRC § 382(l)(3)(A)(i) from the perspective of a loss corporation shareholder here, the result is that sibling shareholders are not aggregated if none of their parents and grandparents is a shareholder of the loss corporation. Accordingly, because Kenneth and Charles were not children or grandchildren of an individual shareholder of Garber (P) at any relevant time, they are not aggregated, so that Charles's purchase of shares from Kenneth in 1998 resulted in an ownership change and the NOL deduction limitations apply. Judgment for the IRS (D).

▶ *ANALYSIS*

As the court mentions in this case, IRC § 382 introduced the concept of an "owner shift." This occurs where the ownership percentage of any individual holding 5% or more of the loss corporation's stock at any time during the three-year testing period increases or decreases as a result of any change in stock ownership. Typically, such a change comes about through a stock purchase. However, owner shifts can occur though certain exchanges, redemptions, stock issuances, or recapitalizations. IRC § 382 expressly excludes owner shifts that are the result of gifts, death, or divorce. Under the IRC, an owner shift is one of two occasions for opening a corporation's stock transfer books to determine whether the aggregate percentage ownership interest of one or more such shareholders has increased by more than 50 percentage

Continued on next page.

points within the relevant lookback period. The other occasion is an "equity structure shift," which includes tax-free reorganizations, certain public offerings, and certain reorganization-like transactions. Either of these occurrences ("owners shift involving 5-percent shareholder" or "equity structure shift") constitutes an "ownership change."

■══■

Quicknotes

TAX DEFICIENCY An unpaid amount of excess tax liability based on a taxpayer's corrected tax amount due less the amount actually paid.

■══■

CHAPTER **14**

Anti-Avoidance Provisions

Quick Reference Rules of Law

Myron's Enterprises v. United States

Corporate taxpayer (P) v. Federal government (D)

548 F.2d 331 (9th Cir. 1977).

NATURE OF CASE: Appeal from grant of partial tax refund.

FACT SUMMARY: The Commissioner (D) contended Myron's Enterprises' (Myron's) (P) retained earnings exceeded its reasonable needs and applied a surtax.

🏛 RULE OF LAW
Accumulated earnings may not exceed the reasonable cost of doing business.

FACTS: Myron's (P) operated a ballroom in a building it leased. It attempted on several occasions to purchase the property, yet was unsuccessful. A third party offered the owner twice as much as Myron's (P) last offer in order to take advantage of the goodwill built up over the years. In order to ensure it would not be bought, Myron's (P) renewed its offer to purchase for each of several years. None of the offers were accepted. The Commissioner (D) assessed a surtax on accumulated income, contending the amount exceeded the reasonable needs of the business. Myron's (P) contended it had to have the large amount of cash available in case the owner was ready to sell. If the building was sold, the business would end. The district court upheld the surtax, while the court of appeals granted a partial refund. Myron's (P) appealed.

ISSUE: May accumulated earnings exceed reasonable costs of doing business?

HOLDING AND DECISION: (Sneed, J.) No. Accumulated earnings may not exceed reasonable costs of doing business. Had the building been sold, Myron's (P) would be out of business. Thus, the availability of cash was reasonably necessary to ensure that a sale could occur. Thus, the accumulated earnings tax was improper. Reversed and remanded.

▶ ANALYSIS

The reasonable business needs test is used to determine if a business is accumulating too much income to avoid tax on a distribution. It is a factual question resolved on a case-by-case basis. If a tax avoidance intent is shown, the reasonableness of the accumulation is placed in question.

■■■

Quicknotes

SURTAX An additional tax applied to something being taxed or applied to the primary tax itself.

■■■

Gazette Publishing Co. v. Self

Corporate taxpayer (P) v. Government official (D)

103 F. Supp. 779 (E.D. Ark. 1952).

NATURE OF CASE: Appeal from imposition of accumulated earnings tax.

FACT SUMMARY: Gazette Publishing Co. (P) purchased a large amount of its own shares at a price above market value to prevent a potential hostile takeover.

RULE OF LAW
Prevention of a sale of corporate stock to a potentially hostile outsider is a legitimate use of corporate earnings.

FACTS: Allsopp was the owner of a significant minority interest in stock of Gazette Publishing Co. (Gazette) (P), publisher of the *Arkansas Gazette*. Allsopp intended to sell the interest. Fearing a threat to its managerial harmony and editorial policy, Gazette (P) agreed to purchase its own stock at a price higher than fair market value. The Internal Revenue Service (IRS) (D) concluded this not to be a legitimate business expenditure and assessed an accumulated earnings tax on the amount. Gazette (P) challenged this in district court.

ISSUE: Is prevention of a sale of corporate stock to a potentially hostile outsider a legitimate use of corporate earnings?

HOLDING AND DECISION: (Trimble, C.J.) Yes. Prevention of a sale of corporate stock to a potentially hostile outsider is a legitimate use of corporate earnings. While there is a personal element in preserving corporate harmony, managerial dissension does indeed pose a threat to a corporation, and the aversion of such a possibility is indeed a legitimate use of corporate funds. To pay more than the fair market value may be proper to ensure that the stock is in fact sold to the corporation. This appears to be the case here. Judgment for Gazette (P).

ANALYSIS

The accumulated earnings tax is a traditional method to compel corporations to reinvest or declare dividends. Since dividends were taxed at the higher individual rates, corporations had an incentive not to declare them. Now, with personal marginal rates much lower in the upper brackets, the need for the tax is probably not so great. In any event, given that corporations may use an accumulated earnings credit that in no event may be lower than the amount by which $250,000 exceeds accumulated earnings and profits at the close of the preceding taxable year, corporations effectively may accumulate a minimum of $250,000 tax-free regardless of business needs.

Quicknotes

FAIR MARKET VALUE The price of particular property or goods that a buyer would offer and a seller would accept in the open market following full disclosure.

HOSTILE TAKEOVER Situation in which an outside group attempts to seize control of a target corporation against the will of the targeted company's officers, directors or shareholders.

The S Corporation

Quick Reference Rules of Law

Harris v. United States

Shareholder (P) v. Federal government (D)

902 F.2d 439 (5th Cir. 1990).

NATURE OF CASE: Appeal from summary dismissal of action for tax refund.

FACT SUMMARY: A bank loaned a start-up company $700,000 to convert a porn theater to a wedding hall; one of the corporation's two shareholders, Harris (P), secured one of its two notes to the bank with a personal certificate of deposit.

🏛 RULE OF LAW
The guarantee of an S corporation's loan by its shareholders is not a capital investment in the company which increases their stock bases for purposes of limiting their deductible losses under IRC § 1366(d).

FACTS: Harris (P) and Martin agreed to buy a pornographic movie theater for the purpose of converting it to a wedding hall, conditioned on their obtaining a third party loan for at least $600,000. They formed Harmar, a subchapter S corporation, to purchase and operate the property, to which they contributed $1,000 each in receipt for its stock. Hibernia Bank loaned Harmar $700,000. Harmar issued Hibernia two promissory notes for $350,000 each; one was secured by two certificates of deposit from Harris (P), the other by Harmar's $3 million note and mortgage on the theater. During 1982, Harmar had a net operating loss of $104,013, half of which was each claimed by Harris (P) and Martin. They claimed that their bases in Harmar stock far exceeded Harmar's loss and that they could deduct their portions of the entire amount. Under IRC § 1366(d), the IRS (D) limited their deductions to their adjusted bases of $1,000 in Harmar stock and $47,500 in Harmar debt.

ISSUE: Does a personal guarantee by shareholders of a loan to a subchapter S corporation increase their bases in the company so that they may have a higher ceiling for deduction of loss under IRC § 1366(d)?

HOLDING AND DECISION: (Garwood, J.) No. A personal guarantee by shareholders of a loan to a subchapter S corporation does not increase their bases in the company so that they may have a higher ceiling for deduction of loss under IRC § 1366(d). IRC § 1366 permits a subchapter S shareholder to deduct from his personal return a proportionate share of the corporation's net operating loss to the extent the loss does not exceed the sum of the adjusted basis of his stock and corporate debt to him. A shareholder must make a true economic outlay to increase basis; a court will not in hindsight recharacterize a guaranteed corporate debt as an equity investment by the shareholder. Accordingly, here shareholders wish to recast Hibernia's $700,000 loan to Harmar as one to them which they in turn contributed to Harmar's capital account, raising their bases and allowing

them to deduct all 1982 losses under § 1366. However, the facts show Harris (P) and Martin intended Hibernia to make the loan directly to Harmar: the notes were in Harmar's name only, the proceeds were used to purchase property in which Harmar held title, the mortgage to secure the loan was given by Harmar, and the corporate records and shareholder personal tax returns show no $700,000 distribution to them and capital contribution to Harmar. Thus, Harris (P) and Martin are limited under IRC § 1366(d) to deducting Harmar losses up to the amount of their respective bases, $48,500. Affirmed.

▶ ANALYSIS

This case aligns the Fifth Circuit with the Fourth and Sixth but is in conflict with the Eleventh, which allowed a determination under Subchapter C debt/equity principles whether a shareholder-guaranteed debt was characterized as a capital contribution. See *Selfe v. United States*, 778 F.2d 769 (11th Cir. 1985). Interestingly, the Supreme Court has refused to resolve this conflict between the Circuits by denying certiorari in an appropriate case. *Estate of Leavitt v. Commissioner*, 875 F.2d 420 (4th Cir. 1989), *cert. denied*, 493 U.S. 958 (1989).

Quicknotes

BASIS The value assigned to a taxpayer's costs incurred as the result of acquiring an asset, and used to compute tax amounts toward the transactions in which that asset is involved.

Joseph Radtke, S.C. v. United States

Corporate taxpayer (P) v. Federal government (D)

712 F. Supp. 143 (E.D. Wis. 1989); *aff'd*, 895 F.2d 1196 (7th Cir. 1990).

NATURE OF CASE: Defense motion for summary judgment in action for refund of payment of tax deficiencies and penalties.

FACT SUMMARY: Radtke (P) was corporate director, sole shareholder, and sole full-time employee of a subchapter S corporation; instead of a salary, he had the company declare dividends payable to him, from which he neglected to deduct Social Security and unemployment compensation taxes.

🏛 RULE OF LAW
Where a subchapter S corporation's sole employee is also its corporate director with the power to declare dividends in lieu of salary, those dividends will be taxed as wages.

FACTS: Radtke (P) was the sole incorporator, shareholder, director, and full-time employee of a subchapter S corporation that provided legal services. Radtke (P) had a base salary of $0, but he collected $18,225 in dividends from the corporation in lieu of salary. Although he paid personal income tax on the dividends, and the company reported the income, the company did not deduct Social Security (FICA) or unemployment (FUTA) taxes. The Internal Revenue Service (D) assessed a deficiency for these amounts. Radtke (P) paid the amounts but then brought suit for a refund. The Government (D) moved for summary judgment.

ISSUE: If the director of a subchapter S corporation, who is also its sole shareholder and only full-time employee, receives dividends in lieu of salary, will those dividends be treated as wages for tax purposes?

HOLDING AND DECISION: (Evans, J.) Yes. If the director of a subchapter S corporation, who is also its sole shareholder and only full-time employee, receives dividends in lieu of salary, those dividends will be treated as wages for tax purposes. The Federal Insurance Contributions Act defines "wages" as "all remuneration for employment." Dividends are not excluded from this definition. Radtke (P) was an employee of his company and as director had the company pay himself as its only significant employee. Looking to the substance rather than the form of the payment to Radtke (P), the dividends were "wages." An employer should not evade FICA or FUTA by characterizing all of an employee's remuneration as something other than "wages." Plaintiff's motion for summary judgment denied and Defendant's motion for summary judgment granted.

▶ ANALYSIS

Subchapter S corporations should also be careful how they treat fringe benefits, such as group medical plans and life insurance policies, for tax purposes. Under IRC § 1372, an S corporation is treated as a partnership for fringe benefit purposes so that a shareholder with more than 2% of the company's stock will be treated as a partner with the result that these fringes seldom are deductible.

■=■

Common Latin Words and Phrases Encountered in the Law

A FORTIORI: Because one fact exists or has been proven, therefore a second fact that is related to the first fact must also exist.

A PRIORI: From the cause to the effect. A term of logic used to denote that when one generally accepted truth is shown to be a cause, another particular effect must necessarily follow.

AB INITIO: From the beginning; a condition which has existed throughout, as in a marriage which was void ab initio.

ACTUS REUS: The wrongful act; in criminal law, such action sufficient to trigger criminal liability.

AD VALOREM: According to value; an ad valorem tax is imposed upon an item located within the taxing jurisdiction calculated by the value of such item.

AMICUS CURIAE: Friend of the court. Its most common usage takes the form of an amicus curiae brief, filed by a person who is not a party to an action but is nonetheless allowed to offer an argument supporting his legal interests.

ARGUENDO: In arguing. A statement, possibly hypothetical, made for the purpose of argument, is one made arguendo.

BILL QUIA TIMET: A bill to quiet title (establish ownership) to real property.

BONA FIDE: True, honest, or genuine. May refer to a person's legal position based on good faith or lacking notice of fraud (such as a bona fide purchaser for value) or to the authenticity of a particular document (such as a bona fide last will and testament).

CAUSA MORTIS: With approaching death in mind. A gift causa mortis is a gift given by a party who feels certain that death is imminent.

CAVEAT EMPTOR: Let the buyer beware. This maxim is reflected in the rule of law that a buyer purchases at his own risk because it is his responsibility to examine, judge, test, and otherwise inspect what he is buying.

CERTIORARI: A writ of review. Petitions for review of a case by the United States Supreme Court are most often done by means of a writ of certiorari.

CONTRA: On the other hand. Opposite. Contrary to.

CORAM NOBIS: Before us; writs of error directed to the court that originally rendered the judgment.

CORAM VOBIS: Before you; writs of error directed by an appellate court to a lower court to correct a factual error.

CORPUS DELICTI: The body of the crime; the requisite elements of a crime amounting to objective proof that a crime has been committed.

CUM TESTAMENTO ANNEXO, ADMINISTRATOR (ADMINISTRATOR C.T.A.): With will annexed; an administrator c.t.a. settles an estate pursuant to a will in which he is not appointed.

DE BONIS NON, ADMINISTRATOR (ADMINISTRATOR D.B.N.): Of goods not administered; an administrator d.b.n. settles a partially settled estate.

DE FACTO: In fact; in reality; actually. Existing in fact but not officially approved or engendered.

DE JURE: By right; lawful. Describes a condition that is legitimate "as a matter of law," in contrast to the term "de facto," which connotes something existing in fact but not legally sanctioned or authorized. For example, de facto segregation refers to segregation brought about by housing patterns, etc., whereas de jure segregation refers to segregation created by law.

DE MINIMIS: Of minimal importance; insignificant; a trifle; not worth bothering about.

DE NOVO: Anew; a second time; afresh. A trial de novo is a new trial held at the appellate level as if the case originated there and the trial at a lower level had not taken place.

DICTA: Generally used as an abbreviated form of obiter dicta, a term describing those portions of a judicial opinion incidental or not necessary to resolution of the specific question before the court. Such nonessential statements and remarks are not considered to be binding precedent.

DUCES TECUM: Refers to a particular type of writ or subpoena requesting a party or organization to produce certain documents in their possession.

EN BANC: Full bench. Where a court sits with all justices present rather than the usual quorum.

EX PARTE: For one side or one party only. An ex parte proceeding is one undertaken for the benefit of only one party, without notice to, or an appearance by, an adverse party.

EX POST FACTO: After the fact. An ex post facto law is a law that retroactively changes the consequences of a prior act.

EX REL.: Abbreviated form of the term ex relatione, meaning upon relation or information. When the state brings an action in which it has no interest against an individual at the instigation of one who has a private interest in the matter.

FORUM NON CONVENIENS: Inconvenient forum. Although a court may have jurisdiction over the case, the action should be tried in a more conveniently located court, one to which parties and witnesses may more easily travel, for example.

GUARDIAN AD LITEM: A guardian of an infant as to litigation, appointed to represent the infant and pursue his/her rights.

HABEAS CORPUS: You have the body. The modern writ of habeas corpus is a writ directing that a person (body) being detained (such as a prisoner) be brought before the court so that the legality of his detention can be judicially ascertained.

IN CAMERA: In private, in chambers. When a hearing is held before a judge in his chambers or when all spectators are excluded from the courtroom.

IN FORMA PAUPERIS: In the manner of a pauper. A party who proceeds in forma pauperis because of his poverty is one who is allowed to bring suit without liability for costs.

INFRA: Below, under. A word referring the reader to a later part of a book. (The opposite of supra.)

IN LOCO PARENTIS: In the place of a parent.

IN PARI DELICTO: Equally wrong; a court of equity will not grant requested relief to an applicant who is in pari delicto, or as much at fault in the transactions giving rise to the controversy as is the opponent of the applicant.

IN PARI MATERIA: On like subject matter or upon the same matter. Statutes relating to the same person or things are said to be in pari materia. It is a general rule of statutory construction that such statutes should be construed together, i.e., looked at as if they together constituted one law.

IN PERSONAM: Against the person. Jurisdiction over the person of an individual.

IN RE: In the matter of. Used to designate a proceeding involving an estate or other property.

IN REM: A term that signifies an action against the res, or thing. An action in rem is basically one that is taken directly against property, as distinguished from an action in personam, i.e., against the person.

INTER ALIA: Among other things. Used to show that the whole of a statement, pleading, list, statute, etc., has not been set forth in its entirety.

INTER PARTES: Between the parties. May refer to contracts, conveyances or other transactions having legal significance.

INTER VIVOS: Between the living. An inter vivos gift is a gift made by a living grantor, as distinguished from bequests contained in a will, which pass upon the death of the testator.

IPSO FACTO: By the mere fact itself.

JUS: Law or the entire body of law.

LEX LOCI: The law of the place; the notion that the rights of parties to a legal proceeding are governed by the law of the place where those rights arose.

MALUM IN SE: Evil or wrong in and of itself; inherently wrong. This term describes an act that is wrong by its very nature, as opposed to one which would not be wrong but for the fact that there is a specific legal prohibition against it (malum prohibitum).

MALUM PROHIBITUM: Wrong because prohibited, but not inherently evil. Used to describe something that is wrong because it is expressly forbidden by law but that is not in and of itself evil, e.g., speeding.

MANDAMUS: We command. A writ directing an official to take a certain action.

MENS REA: A guilty mind; a criminal intent. A term used to signify the mental state that accompanies a crime or other prohibited act. Some crimes require only a general mens rea (general intent to do the prohibited act), but others, like assault with intent to murder, require the existence of a specific mens rea.

MODUS OPERANDI: Method of operating; generally refers to the manner or style of a criminal in committing crimes, admissible in appropriate cases as evidence of the identity of a defendant.

NEXUS: A connection to.

NISI PRIUS: A court of first impression. A nisi prius court is one where issues of fact are tried before a judge or jury.

N.O.V. (NON OBSTANTE VEREDICTO): Notwithstanding the verdict. A judgment n.o.v. is a judgment given in favor of one party despite the fact that a verdict was returned in favor of the other party, the justification being that the verdict either had no reasonable support in fact or was contrary to law.

NUNC PRO TUNC: Now for then. This phrase refers to actions that may be taken and will then have full retroactive effect.

PENDENTE LITE: Pending the suit; pending litigation underway.

PER CAPITA: By head; beneficiaries of an estate, if they take in equal shares, take per capita.

PER CURIAM: By the court; signifies an opinion ostensibly written "by the whole court" and with no identified author.

PER SE: By itself, in itself; inherently.

PER STIRPES: By representation. Used primarily in the law of wills to describe the method of distribution where a person, generally because of death, is unable to take that which is left to him by the will of another, and therefore his heirs divide such property between them rather than take under the will individually.

PRIMA FACIE: On its face, at first sight. A prima facie case is one that is sufficient on its face, meaning that the evidence supporting it is adequate to establish the case until contradicted or overcome by other evidence.

PRO TANTO: For so much; as far as it goes. Often used in eminent domain cases when a property owner receives partial payment for his land without prejudice to his right to bring suit for the full amount he claims his land to be worth.

QUANTUM MERUIT: As much as he deserves. Refers to recovery based on the doctrine of unjust enrichment in those cases in which a party has rendered valuable services or furnished materials that were accepted and enjoyed by another under circumstances that would reasonably notify the recipient that the rendering party expected to be paid. In essence, the law implies a contract to pay the reasonable value of the services or materials furnished.

QUASI: Almost like; as if; nearly. This term is essentially used to signify that one subject or thing is almost analogous to another but that material differences between them do exist. For example, a quasi-criminal proceeding is one that is not strictly criminal but shares enough of the same characteristics to require some of the same safeguards (e.g., procedural due process must be followed in a parole hearing).

QUID PRO QUO: Something for something. In contract law, the consideration, something of value, passed between the parties to render the contract binding.

RES GESTAE: Things done; in evidence law, this principle justifies the admission of a statement that would otherwise be hearsay when it is made so closely to the event in question as to be said to be a part of it, or with such spontaneity as not to have the possibility of falsehood.

RES IPSA LOQUITUR: The thing speaks for itself. This doctrine gives rise to a rebuttable presumption of negligence when the instrumentality causing the injury was within the exclusive control of the defendant, and the injury was one that does not normally occur unless a person has been negligent.

RES JUDICATA: A matter adjudged. Doctrine which provides that once a court of competent jurisdiction has rendered a final judgment or decree on the merits, that judgment or decree is conclusive upon the parties to the case and prevents them from engaging in any other litigation on the points and issues determined therein.

RESPONDEAT SUPERIOR: Let the master reply. This doctrine holds the master liable for the wrongful acts of his servant (or the principal for his agent) in those cases in which the servant (or agent) was acting within the scope of his authority at the time of the injury.

STARE DECISIS: To stand by or adhere to that which has been decided. The common law doctrine of stare decisis attempts to give security and certainty to the law by following the policy that once a principle of law as applicable to a certain set of facts has been set forth in a decision, it forms a precedent which will subsequently be followed, even though a different decision might be made were it the first time the question had arisen. Of course, stare decisis is not an inviolable principle and is departed from in instances where there is good cause (e.g., considerations of public policy led the Supreme Court to disregard prior decisions sanctioning segregation).

SUPRA: Above. A word referring a reader to an earlier part of a book.

ULTRA VIRES: Beyond the power. This phrase is most commonly used to refer to actions taken by a corporation that are beyond the power or legal authority of the corporation.

Addendum of French Derivatives

IN PAIS: Not pursuant to legal proceedings.

CHATTEL: Tangible personal property.

CY PRES: Doctrine permitting courts to apply trust funds to purposes not expressed in the trust but necessary to carry out the settlor's intent.

PER AUTRE VIE: For another's life; during another's life. In property law, an estate may be granted that will terminate upon the death of someone other than the grantee.

PROFIT A PRENDRE: A license to remove minerals or other produce from land.

VOIR DIRE: Process of questioning jurors as to their predispositions about the case or parties to a proceeding in order to identify those jurors displaying bias or prejudice.

Casenote Legal Briefs